CAMPAIGN 318

THE KUBAN 1943

The Wehrmacht's last stand in the Caucasus

ROBERT FORCZYK

ILLUSTRATED BY STEVE NOON
Series editor Marcus Cowper

OSPREY PUBLISHING
Bloomsbury Publishing Plc

Kemp House, Chawley Park, Cumnor Hill, Oxford OX2 9PH, UK
1385 Broadway, 5th Floor, New York, NY 10018, USA
29 Earlsfort Terrace, Dublin 2, Ireland

OSPREY is a trademark of Osprey Publishing, a division of Bloomsbury
Publishing Plc

© 2018 Osprey Publishing – Email: info@ospreypublishing.com

First published in Great Britain in 2018 by Osprey Publishing

A CIP catalogue record for this book is available from the British Library.

ISBN: PB: 978 1 4728 2259 8
             ePub: 978 1 4728 2260 4
             ePDF: 978 1 4728 2261 1
             XML 978 1 4728 2262 8

21 22 23 24 25   10 9 8 7 6 5 4

Index by Alan Rutter
Typeset in Myriad Pro and Sabon
Maps by www.bounford.com
3D BEVs by The Black Spot
Page layouts by PDQ Digital Media Solutions, Bungay, UK
Printed and bound in India by Replika Press Private Ltd.

ACKNOWLEDGEMENTS

I wish to thank Nik Cornish, David Glantz and the staff of the Bundesarchiv
for their help with this project.

ARTIST'S NOTE

Readers may care to note that the original paintings from which the colour
plates in this book were prepared are available for private sale. All
reproduction copyright whatsoever is retained by the Publishers. The artist
can be contacted via the following website:

www.steve-noon.co.uk

The Publishers regret that they can enter into no correspondence upon
this matter.

The Woodland Trust
Osprey Publishing supports the Woodland Trust, the UK's leading woodland
conservation charity.

To find out more about our authors and books visit
www.ospreypublishing.com. Here you will find extracts, author
interviews, details of forthcoming events and the option to sign up for
our newsletter.

LIST OF ACRONYMS AND ABBREVIATIONS

AOK	Armeeoberkommando (Army Command)
BAD	Bombardirovochnaya Aviatsionnaya Diviziya (Bomber Aviation Division)
BAK	Bombardirovochnaya Aviatsionnyi Korpus (Bomber Aviation Corps)
BAP	Bombardirovochnyi Aviatsionnyi Polk (Bomber Aviation Regiment)
CKF	Severo-Kavkazskiy Fronta (North Caucasus Front)
GA	Guards Army
Gd	Guards
GD	Guards Division
GIAP	Gvardeiskyi Isrebitelnyi Aviatsionnyi Polk (Guards Fighter Aviation Regiment)
GMTAP	Gvardeiskyi Minno-Torpednny Aviatsionnyi Polk (Guards Mine-Torpedo Aviation Regiment)
GRD	Guards Rifle Division
GShAP	Gvardeiskyi Shturmovoy Aviatsionnyi Polk (Guards Ground Attack Aviation Regiment)
GTA	Guards Tank Army
HEAT	high-explosive anti-tank
HKL	Hauptkampflinie (Main Line of Resistance)
IAD	Isrebitelnyi Aviatsionnyi Division (Fighter Aviation Division)
IAK	Isrebitelnyi Aviatsionnyi Korpus (Fighter Aviation Corps)
IAP	Isrebitelnyi Aviatsionnyi Polk (Fighter Aviation Regiment)
Jg	Jäger
KG	Kampfgruppe
LBAP	Legko Bombardirovochnyi Aviatsionnyi Polk (Light Bomber Aviation Regiment)
MAS	Mezzi d'Assalto (Assault)
MFP	Marinefährprahme (naval ferry barge)
MTAP	Minno-Torpednny Aviatsionnyi Polk (Mine-Torpedo Aviation Regiment)
NKVD	Narodnyy Komissariat Vnutrennikh Del (People's Commissariat of Internal Affairs)
OBMP	Otdelnyy Batalion Morskoy Pekhoty (Separate Naval Infantry Battalion)
OKH	Oberkommando des Heeres
OTB	Otdel'nyy Tankovyy Batal'on (Independent Tank Battalion)
PzKpfw	Panzerkampfwagen
RO	Romanian
RVGK	Rezerv Verhovnogo Glavnokomandovanija (Stavka Reserve)
SAK	Smeshannyi Aviatsionnyi Korpus (Composite Aviation Corps)
SAP	Smeshannyi Aviatsionnyi Polk (Composite Aviation Regiment)
sFH	schwere Feld Haubitze
ShAD	Shturmovoy Aviatsionnyi Division (Ground Attack Aviation Division)
ShAP	Shturmovoy Aviatsionnyi Polk (Ground Attack Aviation Regiment)
SPW	Schützenpanzerwagen
StuG	Sturmgeschütz
TA	Tank Army
VA	Vozdushnaya Armiya (Air Army)
VMF	Voenno-Morskogo Flota (Military Maritime Fleet)
VVS	Voyenno-Vozdushnye Sily (Military Air Forces)
zbV	zur besonderen Verwendung (Special Purpose)
ZG	Zerstörergeschwader
ZKF	Zakavkazskiy Fronta (Transcaucasus Front)

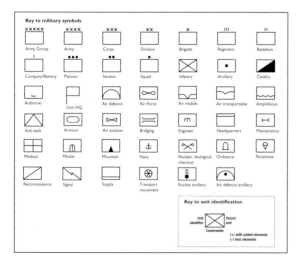

CONTENTS

The German retreat from the Caucasus, 1–31 January 1943

1. 1–19 January 1943: the German LVII Panzerkorps conducts a mobile delaying operation against the Southern Front's 2nd Guards Army, all the way back to the Manych River.
2. 1 January: the Soviet 44th Army conducts a major attack against XXXX Panzerkorps, just as 1.Panzerarmee is about to begin falling back from the Terek.
3. 2–7 January: 1.Panzerarmee withdraws to the Kuma River, where it pauses for four days.
4. 4–12 January: Gruppe Le Suire (4 battalions) retreats from the high mountains.
5. 10 January: Soviet Northern Group eventually breaks through the German defences along the Kuma, forcing 1.Panzerarmee to fall back to the Kalaus Line, where they pause until 17 January.
6. 16–23 January: 56th Army spearheads an offensive by the Black Sea Group of Forces toward Krasnodar, but only advances 20km in a week.
7. 23 January: once across the Manych, the Southern Front links up with the Northern Group's cavalry and threatens to push toward Tikhoretsk to cut 1.Panzerarmee's escape route. Hitler orders von Kleist to send part of 1.Panzerarmee to Rostov, but LII Armeekorps is ordered to the Kuban.
8. 24–31 January: 1.Panzerarmee retreats to Rostov and avoids encirclement. The last units cross the Don on 6 February.
9. 24–31 January: 17.Armee retreats to the Kuban bridgehead.

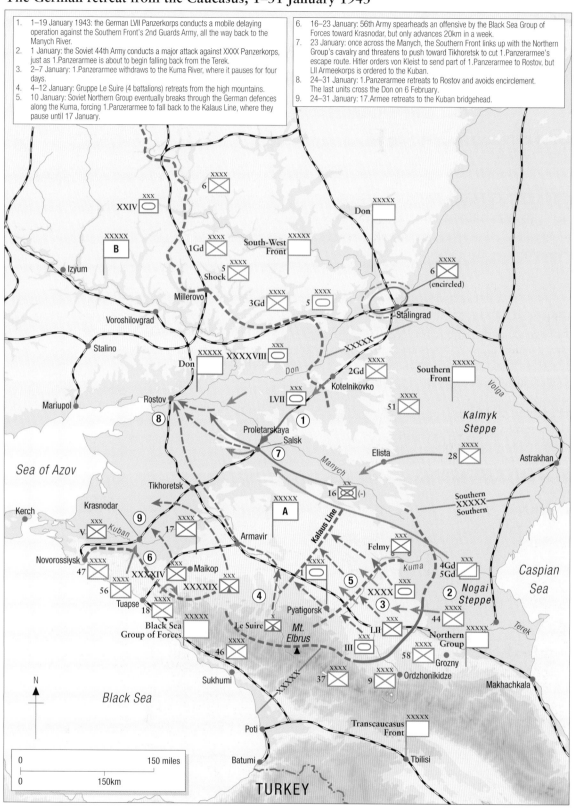

ORIGINS OF THE CAMPAIGN

In April 1942, Hitler announced in his Führer Directive No. 41 that the primary objective of the second German summer offensive in the Soviet Union would be the oilfields in the Caucasus. Three months later, Heeresgruppe Süd (Army Group South) split into two sub-commands, with Heeresgruppe A tasked with the main effort to seize the Caucasus, while Heeresgruppe B would attack towards the Volga to seize Stalingrad. Once Rostov was captured on 23 July, Hitler further clarified his objectives in the Caucasus with Führer Directive No. 45. Operation *Edelweiss*, as the invasion of the Caucasus was designated, intended to use the fast-moving units of Generaloberst Ewald von Kleist's 1.Panzerarmee (PzAOK 1) to seize the Soviet oilfields at Maikop, Grozny and Baku while Generaloberst Richard Ruoff's 17.Armee (AOK 17) cleared the Kuban, the Taman Peninsula and then the Black Sea coast. Back in Berlin, Hitler believed that Heeresgruppe A could advance over 1,000km by the end of the summer, seizing these critical oil-producing areas, which would then be converted to German use. By depriving Stalin of approximately 70 percent of his crude oil production, Hitler believed that *Edelweiss* would decisively cripple the Soviet war effort.

An abandoned PzKpfw III medium tank in January 1943. Note that this tank is outfitted with the wider *Winterketten* (winter tracks). During the retreat from the Caucasus, Heeresgruppe A was forced to abandon a large amount of its vehicles and heavy equipment. Although this tank suffered battle damage, many vehicles were abandoned for lack of fuel. (Bundesarchiv, Bild 101I-328-2911-21, Foto: Siedel)

However, what seemed simple in map exercises proved far more difficult to execute in the field. Heeresgruppe A did succeed in invading the Caucasus in July and quickly routed the armies of the North Caucasus Front. While Kleist's Panzers captured Maikop on 10 August and pushed south towards Grozny, Ruoff overran the Kuban. In the skies, the Fliegerkorps IV gained local air superiority to support the ground offensive. Yet just when Heeresgruppe A appeared to be on the cusp of victory, Hitler began tinkering with the basic plan: he started transferring forces from the Caucasus to reinforce Heeresgruppe B's faltering advance towards the Volga. He also failed to transfer three promised divisions of the Italian Alpine Corps to the Caucasus, where they were desperately needed to help clear the Black Sea coast. By October, Operation *Edelweiss* had run out of steam short of its primary objectives due to increased Soviet resistance and German logistic problems. Ruoff's 17.Armee failed to capture the ports of Tuapse or Sukhumi, despite repeated efforts, and Kleist's 1.Panzerarmee was stopped short of Grozny. One final German push in early November resulted in the near destruction of 13.Panzer-Division when it was briefly encircled.

For a brief period, the front lines in the Caucasus stabilized and both sides shifted to the defensive. In late November, General der Kavallerie Eberhard von Mackensen took command of 1.Panzerarmee while von Kleist moved up to take command of Heeresgruppe A. This brief period of stasis ended when the Soviet South-West and Stalingrad fronts launched a major counter-offensive, Operation *Uranus*, on 19 November 1942. Four days later, the German 6.Armee and part of 4.Panzerarmee in Stalingrad were cut off and faced with destruction. In desperation, the Oberkommando des Heeres (OKH) immediately cobbled together a rescue plan known as Operation *Wintergewitter*, which entailed von Mackensen's 1.Panzerarmee transferring the 23.Panzer-Division and the SS-Panzergrenadier Division Wiking to Generaloberst Hermann Hoth's 4.Panzerarmee. Much of Fliegerkorps IV was also transferred northwards, which immediately gave the Soviet 4th and 5th Air Armies air superiority in the Caucasus.

Heeresgruppe A's position in the Caucasus was quite tenuous and became even worse when Operation *Wintergewitter* failed in mid-December and the Stalingrad Front (renamed the Southern Front on 1 January 1943) began advancing south. It soon became obvious to both sides that Heeresgruppe A might become isolated in the Caucasus; if that occurred, the entire German southern front in Russia would collapse. Yet Hitler was extremely reluctant to abandon his position in the Caucasus and did not authorize a retreat until 29 December; even then, 1.Panzerarmee was only authorized to retreat 100km from the Terek to the Kuma River line. Hitler optimistically believed that the Kuma position could be held until spring 1943, when he could then mount a new offensive towards the Caucasus oilfields. By holding further south, Hitler also hoped to retain the captured oilfields around Maikop, which had just been repaired.

At the end of 1942, Soviet forces in the Caucasus consisted of two main groupings. General-polkovnik Ivan I. Maslennikov's Northern Group of Forces, in the Grozny and Terek River sector, consisted of four armies (9th, 37th, 44th and 58th) and two independent cavalry corps supported by the 4th Air Army (Vozdushnaya Armiya – VA). In the Tuapse sector, General Ivan E. Petrov's Black Sea Group consisted of four armies (18th, 46th, 47th and 56th) supported by the 5th Air Army and the Black Sea Fleet's naval air arm (VVS-ChF). The Transcaucasus Front served as a force provider and logistical source for both groups, but did not directly command units in the field. For the Soviets, the Caucasus was a backwater theatre and received far less material support than was going to the main effort in the Stalingrad sector. Nevertheless, Stavka (the Soviet High Command) expected

A German 15cm infantry gun is towed during the winter retreat. The 17.Armee lost a good portion of its artillery in the retreat to the Kuban and initially was handicapped by severe shortages of food, fuel and ammunition. Hitler made the decision to defend the Kuban bridgehead because he had no real option to withdraw 17.Armee from the Taman Peninsula before spring 1943. (Bundesarchiv, Bild 101I-725-0192-25, Foto: Reimers)

the forces in the Caucasus to drive Heeresgruppe A from the region at the earliest opportunity.

On 1 January 1943, von Mackensen's 1.Panzerarmee began its retreat from the Terek River and Maslennikov's four armies immediately launched their long-planned counter-offensive. Maslennikov's pursuit, spearheaded by two cavalry corps and two ad hoc mechanized groups, was poorly coordinated but managed to keep 1.Panzerarmee on the run and prevent it from forming a viable line on the Kuma River. By 10 January, Maslennikov's spearheads were across the Kuma in force. Even worse for 1.Panzerarmee, the Southern Front pushed Hoth's forces back over 100km and was approaching the Manych River, which threatened to envelop von Mackensen's open left flank. If Soviet armour crossed the river, there would be little to stop it from severing von Mackensen's line of communications and cutting off the bulk of Heeresgruppe A in the Caucasus. Amazingly, Hoth managed to fight a two-week delaying operation on the Manych River, which bought time for von Mackensen's 1.Panzerarmee to escape the Soviet pincers. Overall, the German retreat from the Caucasus was fairly well managed but still something of a disaster since inadequate fuel supplies caused hundreds of vehicles to be abandoned.

Ruoff's 17.Armee was also forced to retreat, which was complicated by the dispersed nature of its forces. The V Armeekorps and the Romanian Cavalry Corps near Novorossiysk were ordered to stand fast, but XXXXIV Armeekorps in the mountains east of Tuapse and XXXXIX Gebirgskorps spread through the mountains north and east of Sukhumi were faced with a daunting retreat through high mountains in winter. All four divisions of the XXXXIV Armeekorps were forced to retreat along the single-track Tuapse–Maikop road, little more than a muddy track, causing great congestion. About half the German artillery and a great deal of ammunition were abandoned during the retreat.

Although Petrov's Black Sea Group was itself short on supplies, Stavka insisted that it begin a counter-offensive against the retreating 17.Armee as soon as possible. (There was no rail link to the Tuapse sector, so the Black

The city of Novorossiysk, viewed from the western side of Tsemes Bay. The Germans occupied the high ridges above the city and everything except the eastern industrial complexes on the right side of the image. The front line in this area was essentially static for an entire year – rare on the Eastern Front. Novorossiysk was one of the main objectives of the Kuban campaign. (Author's collection)

Sea Group had been dependent upon supply by sea for the past six months.) While Petrov favoured a methodical advance over the rough terrain, Marshal Georgy K. Zhukov unrealistically demanded that Petrov mount an all-out offensive to break through to Krasnodar. Petrov dutifully developed a two-phase offensive plan, which he called Operation *More* (*Sea*) and Operation *Gory* (*Mountains*). The first phase began on 12 January 1943 when General-leytenant Fedor V. Kamkov's 47th Army attacked the Romanian Cavalry Corps sector near Krymskaya with two rifle divisions and three brigades. The Romanian 3rd Mountain Division and 9th Infantry Division, holding prepared positions, easily repulsed this inadequate attack and Kamkov was soon relieved of command. Operation *More* was supposed to include an amphibious landing near Novorossiysk, but this was deferred.

Petrov waited a bit longer before implementing Operation *Gory*, but under pressure from Stavka, General-major Andrei A. Grechko's 56th Army began attacking with four rifle divisions in the Severskaya sector, 35km south of Krasnodar, on 16 January 1943. The Romanian 9th Cavalry Division held a 42km-wide front in this sector. With a 5:1 numerical edge in manpower, Grechko's 56th Army was able to surround several Romanian battalions and advanced 10–12km in two days. If Grechko could reach Krasnodar – which was only lightly defended – a good portion of 17.Armee would be isolated. However, persistent rain made tactical mobility difficult in the snow-covered mountains, which gave General der Artillerie Maximilian de Angelis' XXXXIV Armeekorps just enough time to respond to the crisis. Generalleutnant Ernst Rupp's 97.Jäger-Division hurriedly dispatched three battalions to reinforce the Romanian cavalry and German counterattacks on 17–18 January caught Grechko's troops by surprise. Tough infantry combat followed for several days as Rupp's division gradually slowed the 56th Army's advance, assisted by the German 125.Infanterie-Division on one flank and the Slovak 1st (Mobile) Division, which held Goryachy Klyuch. Thanks to Rupp's delaying actions, de Angelis' XXXXIV Armeekorps succeeded in retreating to Krasnodar.

While 17.Armee was doing its best to hold open its retreat routes against persistent Soviet attacks, Hitler was trying to decide upon his course of action in the Caucasus. After the Kuma Line became untenable and the Soviets began crossing the Manych River, it was obvious that Heeresgruppe A could not hold forward positions in the Caucasus. However, Hitler still wanted to retain a foothold in the region in order to keep open options for an offensive in spring 1943 to make another try for the oilfields. Given the parlous state of German forces in southern Russia after the Stalingrad debacle, this was little more than wishful thinking. In Hitler's mind, the Kuban region appeared to offer a defensive bastion that could be held, even though no defensive positions had been prepared. Furthermore, once the Krasnodar–Rostov rail line was cut by the Soviet advance, any German forces in the Kuban would be completely dependent upon air and sea supply, which was inadequate to indefinitely sustain a large force. Initially, Hitler ordered both 1.Panzerarmee and 17.Armee to retreat into the Kuban, which the OKH quickly recognized as a disaster, since the Soviet Southern Front could then easily capture Rostov and push westwards towards the Donbass.

This was one of the key strategic decisions that Hitler made in the campaign in Russia and as usual he chose a compromise that satisfied no one. Hitler agreed to allow just two of 1.Panzerarmee's six remaining divisions to retreat to Rostov, but LII Armeekorps, 13.Panzer-Division and the 2nd Mountain Division (Romanian) were ordered to join Ruoff's 17.Armee in the Kuban. If the 19 Axis divisions consigned to a cul-de-sac in the Kuban had been withdrawn to the Donbass region instead, Generalfeldmarschall Erich von Manstein's Heeresgruppe Don would have been better equipped to hold the Soviet advances towards Kharkov. However, this fleeting opportunity evaporated on 30 January when the Soviet 9th Army captured the town of Tikhoretsk, which severed the Rostov–Krasnodar rail link and thereby isolated 17.Armee in the Kuban.

It is amazing that even before the encircled 6.Armee had surrendered at Stalingrad, Hitler was consigning another German army to isolation in the Kuban. Yet it should be noted that Hitler had few options in January 1943. It would have been virtually impossible for 17.Armee to withdraw northwards to Rostov before Soviet armour arrived and cut off their escape route. The only divisions in 1.Panzerarmee that succeeded in escaping along this route were motorized, but Ruoff's army consisted primarily of non-motorized units. Nor was a Dunkirk-style evacuation across the Kerch Strait feasible due to the winter weather and limited Kriegsmarine transport assets available; at best, the bulk of 17.Armee could not be evacuated by sea until spring 1943. Consequently, Hitler now had little choice but to order 17.Armee to fight a delaying action in the Kuban.

General der Gebirgstruppe Rudolf Konrad's XXXXIX Gebirgskorps brought up the rear in the retreat of Heeresgruppe A to the Kuban. Oberstleutnant Alfons Auer from Grenadier-Regiment 42, 46.Infanterie-Division, was chosen to lead the rearguard, preventing the pursuing Soviets from cutting off the trailing units. On the night of 30/31 January 1943, Kampfgruppe Auer crossed the Ust-Labinskaya Bridge over the frozen Kuban River with Soviet tanks in hot pursuit and the bridge was blown up. The German defence of the Kuban had begun.

In order to hold the Kuban bridgehead, the Luftwaffe was forced to scramble to organize another airlift just after the failure of the Stalingrad one. Since few Ju-52 transports were left operational, 18 Do-24T flying boats from Seenotstaffel 7 and Seenotstaffel 8 were pressed into service to ferry supplies to the Taman Peninsula. Due to the poor condition of Kuban airstrips in the spring thaw, the Dorniers often landed in the waters of Lake Vitzayevskiy near the port of Anapa. Normally the Do-24T could only carry 24 troops or about 3 tons of cargo, but in a pinch it could carry 50 troops for short distances. (Author's collection)

CHRONOLOGY

1942

9 August — 17.Armee captures Krasnodar.

2 September — German forces begin crossing the Kerch Strait.

10 September — The 17.Armee captures Novorossiysk.

23 October — The 17.Armee's offensive toward Tuapse fails to achieve its objective.

29 December — Hitler authorizes 1.Panzerarmee to begin a limited retreat.

1943

1 January — Heeresgruppe A begins to retreat from the Caucasus.

12 January — The Soviet 47th Army counterattacks toward Novorossiysk in Operation *More* (*Sea*).

16 January — The Soviet Black Sea Group begins its counter-offensive with Operation *Gory* (*Mountains*).

24 January — Hitler orders 17.Armee to withdraw into the Kuban bridgehead.

30 January — Tikhoretsk is lost, severing the Rostov–Krasnodar rail link.

31 January — The 17.Armee successfully retreats into the Kuban.

4 February — The Soviets conduct amphibious landings near Novorossiysk.

9 February — The Soviets begin the Krasnodar offensive.

12 February — The Red Army liberates Krasnodar.

20 February — The Azov Flotilla reforms at Yeisk.

7 March — Hitler orders the Organization Todt to begin building a 6km-long bridge across the Kerch Strait.

4–28 April — First Soviet Kuban offensive begins.

17 April — German Operation *Neptun* against the Myskhako bridgehead.

29 April–4 May — Second Soviet Kuban offensive.

4 May — Germans abandon Krymskaya.

26 May — Third Soviet Kuban offensive.

10 September — Soviet landing operation in Novorossiysk.

12 September — The 17.Armee begins evacuating from the Kuban.

16 September — The Red Army liberates Novorossiysk.

21 September — Anapa is liberated.

9 October — The last German troops evacuate from the Taman Peninsula.

OPPOSING COMMANDERS

AXIS

Generaloberst Richard Ruoff (1883–1967) took command of 17.Armee on 1 June 1942. Ruoff was a career infantry officer with extensive command and staff experience in both world wars. During the opening phase of the war, in 1939–41, Ruoff led V Armeekorps, then commanded 4.Panzerarmee in early 1942. His leadership of 17.Armee during the Caucasus campaign in 1942 was uninspired and failed to capture Tuapse, although he succeeded in conducting a successful defence of the Kuban bridgehead. Hitler relieved Ruoff of command in June 1943, sending him to the Führer Reserve; he received no further assignments during the war. Ruoff proved to be an able corps commander but was promoted above his level of ability.

 Generaloberst Erwin Jaenecke (1890–1960) took command of 17.Armee in the Kuban bridgehead on 24 June 1943. Jaenecke came from the *Pioniere* and saw little combat in World War I or the first two years of World War II, nor did he have significant command experience. In February 1942, he was a staff officer in Paris when he was picked to lead 389.Infanterie-Division in the summer offensive in southern Russia. Jaenecke's division was destroyed at Stalingrad and he was badly wounded, but flown out in January 1943. He was sent to recover in France, commanding a corps, then returned to the Eastern Front to take over 17.Armee in the Kuban. Jaenecke was a poor choice as an army commander, having limited command experience and his attitude rapidly deteriorated into pessimism. Hitler would blame him for the loss of the Crimea in May 1944, and his subsequent court martial ended his rather undistinguished military career.

 General der Artillerie Maximilian de Angelis (1889–1974) took command of XXXXIV Armeekorps in January 1942. De Angelis was commissioned in the Austro-Hungarian Army as an artillery officer in 1910 and served on the Eastern and Italian fronts. He remained in Austrian military service after World War I, but became an ardent Nazi in the 1930s and conspired to aid the Germans during the 1938 Anschluss. Transferring to the Wehrmacht, de Angelis commanded 76.Infanterie-Division during 1939–41 but saw relatively little combat. This changed in 1942, when he led XXXXIV Armeekorps into the Caucasus. After the Kuban campaign, he commanded 6.Armee then 2.Panzerarmee in 1944–45. He surrendered to US troops in 1945 but was eventually handed over to the Soviets and remained in captivity until 1955.

Generaloberst Richard Ruoff, commander of 17.Armee in the Kuban. Ruoff was able to conduct a competent defence in the Kuban, but Hitler relieved him of command in June 1943 after Ruoff kept requesting to withdraw his army. His successor, Generaloberst Erwin Jaenecke, also requested evacuation. (Author's collection)

General der Gebirgstruppe Rudolf Konrad (1891–1964) became commander of XXXXIX Gebirgskorps in December 1941. Konrad served as an artillery officer in the Bavarian Army during World War I and was retained in the post-war Reichswehr. He served as a staff officer during 1939–41, but helped organize the new 7.Gebirgs-Division in Germany and was then given a corps command. He led his corps in the Caucasus and the Kuban, until it was destroyed in the Crimea in 1944. Konrad later commanded a corps in Hungary in 1945 but was fortunate to escape Soviet captivity.

General der Infanterie Wilhelm Wetzel (1888–1964) took command of V Armeekorps in January 1942. Wetzel had a distinguished record as a junior infantry officer in World War I and was retained in the Reichswehr. He commanded the 255.Infanterie-Division in the French campaign and *Barbarossa*. He commanded V Armeekorps in the Caucasus and the Kuban, but resigned his command on 1 July 1943 and spent much of the rest of the war in the Führer Reserve.

SOVIET

The Soviet command structure in the Kuban campaign was often confusing, with the Transcaucasus Front responsible for part of the sector and the North Caucasus Front for the rest. Adding to the confusion, Soviet army-level commands in the Kuban frequently played 'musical chairs', with the same group of generals shuffled around every few months, often for reasons that available sources do not reveal.

Marshal Georgy K. Zhukov arrived in the Caucasus on 18 April as a senior Stavka representative, and had a major impact on the planning of the North Caucasus Front's offensives. He remained in the Caucasus until 12 May and probably played a major role in replacing Maslennikov with Petrov.

General-polkovnik Ivan I. Maslennikov (1900–54) took over the North Caucasus Front on 24 January 1943. Maslennikov joined the Bolsheviks in 1917 and served as a cavalry leader in the Caucasus and Central Asia. In 1928, he transferred from the Red Army to the NKVD Border Troops and became a close associate of NKVD chief Lavrentiy Beria. In July 1941, Maslennikov was given command of the 29th Army in the Western Front, then was shifted to command the 39th Army during the Moscow counter-offensive. Maslennikov's 39th Army pushed far into the German rear areas south-west of Rzhev but soon found itself encircled and his army was destroyed by June 1942. Shifted to the Caucasus Front following that debacle, Maslennikov took command of the Northern Group of Forces, which attempted to delay 1.Panzerarmee's advance to the Terek River. When the Soviet counter-offensive began in January 1943, Maslennikov's pursuit was slow and allowed Heeresgruppe A to escape from the Caucasus without severe losses. Maslennikov lacked the experience and skill for large-formation command and owed his appointment to his ties with Beria, but his performance in the Kuban was poor and he was eventually replaced after numerous failures. Nevertheless, Maslennikov was given other major commands and his career was successful until Beria's fall in 1953. Faced with probable trial for his role in NKVD crimes, Maslennikov committed suicide.

General Ivan E. Petrov was initially Maslennikov's deputy and succeeded him. Petrov was a more experienced commander, but his offensives were not successful either. He was a solid but uninspired commander. (Author's collection)

General Ivan E. Petrov (1896–1958) took command of the Black Sea Group of Forces in October 1942. Petrov was an experienced commander who led the independent Coastal Army during the Crimean campaign in 1941–42. After his command was destroyed at Sevastopol in June 1942, Petrov took over the 44th Army in the Caucasus and in October 1942 he assumed command of the Black Sea Group of Forces. In March 1943, he became Maslennikov's chief of staff and then replaced him as front commander on 13 May. While Petrov was a superior commander to Maslennikov, he was not a risk-taker and was best suited to positional warfare where the Red Army could employ its superior numbers and firepower to grind the Germans down. Petrov was demoted in 1944 but managed to later serve as a front commander in the Ukraine.

General-mayor Andrei A. Grechko (1903–76) took command of the 56th Army on 5 January 1943. Grechko was a Ukrainian cavalry officer who was trained as a General Staff officer during the interwar period. He was an ardent communist and used his party contacts to further his career. In the last eight months of 1942, Grechko commanded three different armies in the Caucasus and had a penchant for replacing commanders who had been relieved. Grechko was a competent commander, but no more. He also tended to exaggerate his accomplishments. Nonetheless, he had a very successful military career and served as Minister of Defence from 1967 to 1976.

The 40-year-old General-mayor Andrei A. Grechko played major roles in both the Caucasus and Kuban campaigns. His history of the campaign, written in the 1960s after he was defence minister, reflected the official Soviet view of the campaign and exaggerated the Red Army's battlefield accomplishments in the Kuban. (Author's collection)

General-mayor Ivan A. Rubanyuk (1896–1959) took over command of the 10th Guards Rifle Corps at the start of the Kuban campaign. Rubanyuk was born near Brest and was drafted into the Russian Imperial Army in 1915. He served for two years in the elite Egersky Guards Regiment and was made an NCO. When the Russian Civil War broke out, Rubanyuk joined the Red Army but was soon assigned to a special Cheka battalion in the Ukraine from 1920 to 1923; he undoubtedly participated in the Red Terror in that region. Returning to the regular army, Rubanyuk rose to command a rifle regiment but he was purged in 1937. Three years later, Rubanyuk was reinstated as a regimental commander. In July 1942, he commanded the 176th Rifle Division during the Caucasus campaign and performed well enough to be made a corps commander in October. Rubanyuk was at the forefront of the Soviet efforts to penetrate the German Blue Line. He remained in command of the 10th Guards Rifle Corps until the end of the war.

OPPOSING FORCES

AXIS

Armour

The Germans had very little armour in the Kuban. Generalmajor Hellmut von der Chevallerie's decimated 13.Panzer-Division reached the Kuban with just 11 operational PzKpfw IV medium tanks in two small companies under Hauptmann Hans-Georg von Gusovius. The division's *Gepanzert* (armoured infantry battalion), Hauptmann Waldemar von Gazen's I./Panzergrenadier-Regiment 66, only had one company mounted on half-tracks, with a total of just 17 SPWs (Schützenpanzerwagen). Since most of the divisional artillery had been abandoned in the retreat, II./Panzer-Artillerie-Regiment 13 was the only effective artillery unit left, with eight 10.5cm and four 15cm guns. Not only was 13.Panzer-Division much reduced, but 17.Armee decided to use what was left in small *Kampfgruppen*, rather than as a concentrated *Panzer-Division*. Kampfgruppe Brux was the strongest and usually had the remaining Panzers, mobile infantry and artillery; it usually supported Gruppe Angelis (XXXXIV Armeekorps). Smaller formations like Kampfgruppe Ratzel (400 troops from the *Pioniere*, *Kradschützen* and reconnaissance battalion) were assigned to support XXXXIX Gebirgskorps. Kampfgruppe Polster consisted of just I./Panzergrenadier-Regiment 93 and tended to support V Armeekorps, while II/Panzergrenadier-Regiment 66 was kept as a reserve in the Taman Peninsula. By April, 13.Panzer-Division still only had 19 operational tanks (1 PzKpfw II, 3 PzKpfw III [short], 12 PzKpfw III [Long], 2 PzKpf IV [long] and 1 PzBef) but gained two additional artillery batteries. It was not until May that 30 new PzKpfw IV tanks arrived in the Kuban, but then the division began withdrawing piecemeal to the Crimea in June. When the last elements of 13.Panzer-Division left the Kuban in July, the OKH provided 17.Armee with 15 captured French tanks as substitutes.

Panzerjäger-Abteilung 525 was 17.Armee's only mobile anti-tank reserve and was equipped with two companies of Marder II tank destroyers and one company of towed anti-tank guns. The Marder II combined the new 7.5cm PaK gun on top of a PzKpfw II light tank chassis. The Marder II was a formidable defensive weapon and accounted for large numbers of Soviet tanks in the Kuban. (Author's collection)

The 17.Armee also had two assault gun battalions, each with about 15 Sturmgeschütz (StuG) IIIs left. Ruoff also split these units up, deploying individual batteries to threatened sectors. Ruoff kept Panzerjäger-Abteilung 525, which had two companies of Marder II tank destroyers, as his main anti-tank reserve. It was fortunate for 17.Armee that the Soviets had relatively few tanks in the Kuban, since the infantry division's anti-tank guns were mostly 3.7cm and 5cm PaK. The handful of 7.5cm anti-tank guns were all PaK 97/38 pieces that fired HEAT ammunition. The Romanian Army also managed to contribute some armour to the Kuban. In May 1943, an armoured battalion was formed in the Crimea equipped with 50 Czech-built PzKpfw 38(t) light tanks (designated T-38 in Romanian service). In late July, this battalion was sent to join the Romanian Cavalry Corps in the Kuban and fought in the later stages of the campaign.

In May 1943, the Romanian Army sent a tank battalion to the Kuban equipped with Czech-built Pz 38(t) light tanks (designated T-38 in Romanian service). Since the Soviets did not have many T-34 tanks in the Kuban, obsolescent tanks like this could still be used to support local counterattacks. (Süddeutsche Zeitung, 00404162)

Infantry

The German defence of the Kuban rested upon the quality of its infantry, which were in decline, but still formidable. For example, in early February, 73.Infanterie-Division retained a nine infantry battalion structure and had a combat strength of 8,600 with an additional 2,539 Hiwis (former Soviet prisoners who volunteered to serve in the Wehrmacht). In material terms, the division still possessed 96 per cent of its artillery and 88 per cent of its machine guns. For transport, the division had 4,500 horses and about 400 motor vehicles. On the other end of the scale, 50.Infanterie-Division had been badly chewed up in the Caucasus campaign and was reduced to just six depleted infantry battalions. German infantry battalions in the Kuban averaged about 250 troops, equivalent to only one-third of their authorized strength. In addition to standard infantry divisions, 17.Armee also had two *Jäger-Divisionen* and two *Gebirgs-Divisionen*, each of which possessed two infantry regiments with three battalions each. The 5.Luftwaffen-Feld-Division was even smaller, with just four infantry battalions.

German Gebirgsjäger manning a heavy machine gun in the Kuban, summer 1943. The German defence was based on the tight integration of obstacles, automatic weapons and artillery support – just as it had been in 1918 on the Western Front. The Gebirgsjäger were elite and well-conditioned troops. (Nik Cornish at www.Stavka.org.uk)

The 17.Armee was low on the list for infantry replacements and found it difficult to replace both combat and non-combat losses. For example, 97.Jäger-Division started the campaign with a *Gefechtsstärke* (fighting strength) of 4,640 troops and suffered 1,594 casualties and 751 sick by the end of March, reducing the total strength by 2,345 men, but received only 2,219 replacements. The situation improved by June 1943, with more replacements

arriving to stay ahead of attrition losses, but infantry battalions rarely achieved more than 50 per cent of their authorized strength. In another indication that they were last on the priority list, the OKH decided to suspend shipping new MG 42 machine guns to 17.Armee and instead they received more captured weaponry. By June 1943, about 20–30 per cent of 17.Armee's infantry weapons were non-operational due to lack of spare parts.

Support units

The 17.Armee was not one of the better-equipped formations on the Eastern Front and had not really been configured for independent operations. Rather, 17.Armee had been established to conduct mopping-up operations in the Caucasus against poorly equipped Soviet formations. Most of the transport was horse-drawn and a large amount of the motor transport was lost in the retreat to the Kuban. By June 1943, only 10–20 per cent of the trucks and motor vehicles were operational, so the dependence upon horse transport increased further. In order to reduce wear and tear on trucks, German *Pioniere* built a narrow-gauge rail line from Taman to near the front lines, ensuring that at least food and ammunition could move to forward areas.

On the positive side, 17.Armee did have a dozen corps-level artillery battalions, including two equipped with 21cm Mörser, plus three battalions of Nebelwerfer rocket launchers. However, since many of the prime movers had been lost in the retreat to the Kuban, the artillery was not very mobile. Nor was much artillery ammunition available until May. On the negative side, 17.Armee only had a single army-level *Panzerjäger* unit, three *Pionier Bataillonen* and a couple of Flak battalions.

Romanian forces

The Romanian presence in the Kuban was considerable – six divisions with 64,000 troops – and it was the only place on the Eastern Front in 1943 where an Axis ally was still playing a significant combat role. When well supported by artillery and provided with effective anti-tank defences, Romanian troops proved far more capable of holding ground in the Kuban than they had been in the open steppes around Stalingrad. Formations such as the 3rd Mountain

Romanian infantrymen defending a reverse slope position in the Kuban, probably in the Krymskaya sector. The Romanian Army played a major role in holding the Kuban, the last sector where an Axis ally made a useful contribution on the Eastern Front. Although some German officers criticized Romanian morale at times, most units proved stubborn in the defence when they had proper air and artillery support. (Süddeutsche Zeitung, 00404157)

Division (infantry), over 10,000 strong, were quite capable and well regarded by the Germans. During the winter of 1942/43, the Romanian units in the Caucasus were reinforced with an infusion of German equipment, including heavier artillery, 5cm and 7.5cm anti-tank guns, sub-machine guns and 400 MG 42 machine guns. The Royal Romanian Air Force also occasionally operated over the Kuban, including IAR-80 fighters from the 3rd Fighter Group. In the summer of 1943, the Germans also provided some Ju-87 Stukas to the Romanians, who sent a dive-bombing group to support 17.Armee.

Nevertheless, Romanian morale was fragile after Stalingrad and the Germans were often reluctant to use their troops in critical sectors. In the Kuban, the Germans often formed mixed *Kampfgruppen* that included Romanian battalions and companies, which was highly unusual. The 17.Armee did this because it was increasingly short of German infantry, but also to enhance the staying power of Romanian units when fighting alongside German troops.

The Ju-87 Stuka dive-bomber was still quite useful in the Kuban and the presence of several Stuka *Gruppen* played a major role in thwarting the Soviet offensives between April and June 1943. Indeed, Luftwaffe support was critical in enabling 17.Armee to fend off repeated powerful Soviet offensives. (Nik Cornish at www.Stavka.org.uk)

Luftwaffe

After Fliegerkorps IV left the Caucasus, the Luftwaffe only had minor forces in the region until April 1943. At that point, with much of the rest of the Eastern Front relatively quiet, the Luftwaffe began shifting Fliegerkorps I back into the Crimea to support 17.Armee's defence of the Kuban. In April 1943, four Stuka *Gruppen* from Sturzkampfgeschwader 2 and Sturzkampfgeschwader 77 arrived in Kerch with nearly 150 Ju-87D dive-bombers and were soon joined by six bomber *Gruppen* with nearly 200 Ju-88s and He-111s. Three *Staffeln* from II./Schlachtgeschwader 1 were also based at Anapa with 23 Fw-190A-5 fighter-bombers and 15 Hs-123B ground attack planes. This infusion of airpower provided 17.Armee with powerful close air support just as the North Caucasus Front was beginning its main spring offensive. Furthermore, the Jagdflieger of Jagdgeschwader 3 and Jagdgeschwader 52 had some of the best German fighter pilots available and they inflicted heavy losses on the VVS in April and May 1943 over the Kuban.

A Lend Lease Grant/Lee medium tank burns after another unsuccessful Soviet attack in the Kuban. Most of the Soviet tanks used in the first few Kuban offensives were Lend-Lease American and British vehicles, and few T-34s were ever available to the North Caucasus Front. (Author's collection)

However, the Luftwaffe presence in the Crimea and the Kuban was ephemeral and when most was withdrawn to support Operation *Zitadelle* against the Kursk salient, the Soviets regained air superiority over the Kuban.

SOVIET

Armour

The Red Army started the Kuban campaign with about 275 tanks, spread out among four tank brigades, a tank regiment and nine independent tank battalions (Otdel'nyy Tankovyy Batal'on –

OTB), all operating in the infantry support role. More than two-thirds of the tanks had been provided by Lend-Lease (approximately 70 M3 Lees, 70 Valentines, 30 M3 Stuarts and nine M4A2 Shermans). There were only a handful of T-34s in the Kuban region in February 1943 and the only other Soviet-built tanks were small numbers of T-26 and T-60 light tanks. In addition, the Red Army managed to repair at least 13 German tanks (nine PzKpfw III and four PzKpfw IV) abandoned in the retreat from the Caucasus and these were pressed into service. Soviet armour in the Kuban was not concentrated into corps-size formations, but instead dispersed in the infantry support role.

Belatedly, Stavka began to improve the quality of the North Caucasus Front's armour in May 1943 by disbanding most of the OTBs and their motley collection of tanks and sending several larger, better-equipped armoured units to the region. Five new tank regiments arrived, each with about 20–40 tanks, including two equipped with T-34/76 tanks and the 6th Guards Tank Regiment with 21 KV-1 heavy tanks. Two self-propelled artillery regiments also arrived, each with 8 Su-76 and 12 Su-122 guns. Once these reinforcements were integrated, the North Caucasus Front had about 400 tanks and assault guns to support their offensives, but still without any real armoured mass.

Infantry

The rifle brigade, rather than the rifle division, was the Red Army's primary tactical unit in the Kuban. On paper, the rifle brigade was authorized over 4,100 troops and was designed to conduct independent missions; it had more organic firepower than the 2,400-man rifle regiment in a rifle division. For example, about 15 per cent of the troops in rifle brigades carried sub-machine guns, whereas the infantry in the standard rifle units still relied on the bolt-action Mosin–Nagant rifle. When three brigades were grouped into a rifle corps, their manpower strength and firepower were usually equivalent to a reinforced rifle division. Soviet commanders criticized the performance of their infantry in the Kuban, noting that they tended to advance in a herd, were difficult to control on the battlefield and failed to dig in quickly after seizing an objective. Soviet infantry firepower was also assessed by General Petrov as 'extremely insufficient' compared to German firepower; this seems odd given the amount of automatic weapons and mortars available but the likely interpretation is that inadequate training prevented the Soviet infantry from getting the most out of their weapons. Many Soviet troops who served in the Kuban were recent conscripts, hastily thrown into battle.

The Soviet 10th and 11th Guards Rifle corps were the two primary assault formations in the 56th Army and by May 1943 they had a solid core of veteran Guards Rifle brigades assigned. The Guards Rifle units usually had a higher percentage of sub-machine gunners than standard Soviet infantry units, which still relied on the bolt-action Mosin–Nagant rifle. (Courtesy of the Central Museum of the Armed Forces, Moscow via Stavka)

The Red Army employed a number of mountain rifle units in the Kuban. Most of these formations were based upon pre-war regular units and some still retained old-style organizations, such as five companies within a mountain rifle regiment. By 1943, a mountain rifle regiment at authorized strength could employ two rifle battalions, each with about 450 troops, supported by four 76mm mountain guns and four 107mm mortars. Of course, Red Army units were rarely at authorized strength and were fortunate to have 70–80 per cent of authorized strength at the start of an operation, which quickly dwindled to 30 per cent or so after a few weeks of combat.

The Black Sea Fleet contributed two naval rifle brigades and three naval rifle battalions, totaling about 10,000 sailors, to the Kuban campaign. The naval rifle units were quite large, with a battalion authorized over 1,000 troops, and a three-battalion brigade at full strength approached 4,000 troops. Although Soviet naval infantry had no special training, they were generally regarded as tough troops with excellent morale.

Soviet Military Aviation (VVS) support

At the beginning of the Soviet winter counter-offensive in the Caucasus, the Soviets enjoyed a 9:1 numerical superiority in the air over the retreating German armies. Yet since this region was a secondary theatre, the 4th Vozdushnaya Armiya (VA – Air Army), 5th VA and VVS-ChF were still operating some older aircraft like the I-16 and I-153 fighters in early 1943, along with SB bombers. In January 1943, Stavka transferred 60 LaGG-3 fighters and 20 Il-2 Sturmoviks to provide some newer aircraft to the VVS in this theatre. However, once the Luftwaffe returned in force to the region, Stavka decided to transfer over 300 modern aircraft to reinforce the 4th VA and 5th VA to support the offensive against the Blue Line. These reinforcements included four regiments of La-5 fighters and ten regiments of Yak-1 and Yak-7 fighters. By May 1943, the VVS had nearly 500 fighters operating in the Kuban region, although many units only remained in theatre for a few weeks.

The VVS in the Kuban also benefited from a steady stream of Lend-Lease aircraft provided through the Persian corridor, established by the Western Allies in December 1942.

In January 1943, three Soviet regiments began transitioning to the P-39 Airacobra fighter, while two regiments trained on the British Spitfire Mk Vb. Lend-Lease aircraft played a significant role in VVS operations over the Kuban. The VVS also deployed a large number of Il-2 Sturmovik ground attack aircraft and Pe-2 bombers to the Caucasus, which constantly harassed German positions.

The VVS-ChF contributed about 150 aircraft to support operations along the Black Sea coast, of which the most significant were the A-20C Bostons of 36th Mine-Torpedo Aviation Regiment (Minno-Torpednny Aviatsionnyi Polk – MTAP) and the Il-4s of 5th Guards Mine-Torpedo Aviation Regiment (Gvardeiskyi Minno-Torpednny Aviatsionnyi Polk – GMTAP), since these aircraft were best suited for air–sea interdiction missions. The Soviet Navy had perfected the AMG-1 air-delivered contact mine in 1940 and aerial-delivered torpedoes, which could be delivered by A-20s and Il-4s. By 1943, the VVS-ChF had the technology and the experienced pilots needed to interdict enemy naval traffic to the Kuban.

GERMAN

HEERESGRUPPE A (GENERALFELDMARSCHALL EWALD VON KLEIST)

17.Armee (Generaloberst Richard Ruoff)

V Armeekorps (General der Infanterie Wilhelm Wetzel)
- 9.Infanterie-Division (Generalleutnant Siegmund Freiherr von Schleinitz)
- 73.Infanterie-Division (Generalleutnant Rudolf von Bünau)
- 5.Luftwaffen-Feld-Division (Oberst Hans-Bruno Schulz-Heyn)
- Sturmgeschütz-Abteilung 249 (Major Kurt Schäff)
- 3rd Mountain Division (Romanian)
- 10th Infantry Division (Romanian)
- Artillerie-Abteilung 634 (10cm)
- Artillerie-Abteilung 737 (Czech 14.9mm sFH 37(t) howitzers)
- Artillerie-Abteilung 767 (15cm)

Gruppe Angelis (XXXXIV Armeekorps) (General der Artillerie Maximilian de Angelis)

- 97.Jäger-Division (Generalleutnant Ernst Rupp)[1]
- 101.Jäger-Division (Generalleutnant Emil Vogel)
- 125.Infanterie-Division
- 198.Infanterie-Division
- Romanian Cavalry Corps
  - 6th Cavalry Division (Romanian)
  - 9th Cavalry Division (Romanian)
  - 19th Infantry Division (Romanian)
  - Corps Artillery Regiment
- Artillerie-Abteilung 151 (10cm)
- 2.Batterie/Artillerie-Abteilung 767 (15cm)
- 2.Batterie, II./Artillerie-Regiment 77 (15cm)
- 6.Batterie/Artillerie-Lehr-Regiment 2

XXXXIX Gebirgskorps (General der Gebirgstruppe Rudolf Konrad)

- 1.Gebirgs-Division
- 4.Gebirgs-Division
- 46.Infanterie-Division
- Radfahrer-Regiment 4[2]
- Artillerie-Abteilung 154 (Czech 14.9mm sFH 37(t) howitzers)
- II./Artillerie-Regiment 42 (15cm)
- schwere Artillerie-Abteilung 732 (21cm Mörser)

LII Armeekorps (General der Infanterie Eugen Ott)

- 50.Infanterie-Division
- 370.Infanterie-Division
- 13.Panzer-Division (Generalmajor Hellmut von der Chevallerie)
- 2nd Mountain Division (Romanian)
- Sturmgeschütz-Abteilung 191 (Hauptmann Wolfgang Kapp)
- Panzerjäger-Abteilung 525 (Marder II)
- Radfahr-Abteilung 45
- II./Artillerie-Regiment 60 (10cm)
- II./Artillerie-Regiment 65 (1 x 10cm, 2 x 15cm batteries)
- schwere Artillerie-Abteilung 602 (1 x 10cm, 2 x 15cm batteries)
- schwere Artillerie-Abteilung 844 (15cm)
- 1.Batterie/Artillerie-Regiment 711 (10cm)
- schwere Artillerie-Abteilung 207 (21cm Mörser)
- I./Werfer-Regiment 52
- II., III./Werfer-Regiment 1[3]

Under 17.Armee:

- Slovak 1st (Mobile) Division[4]
- Flak-Regiment 42

Grenadier-Bataillon zbV 560

LUFTWAFFE

III./Jagdgeschwader 52 (Bf-109G)
13./Jagdgeschwader 52 (Slovak) (Bf-109F)

KRIEGSMARINE

1.Landungs-Flotille (Marinefährprahme – MFP)
3.Landungs-Flotille (MFP)
3.Räumbootsflotille (Kapitänleutnant Klassmann): R36, R37, R163, R165, R166
1.Schnellbootsflotille (Korvettenkapitän Georg-Stuhr Christiansen): S-26, S-27, S-28, S-40, S-47, S-51, S-72, S-102

REGIA MARINA (ITALY)

4ª Flottiglia MAS (Commander Francesco Mimbelli): 8 boats

REINFORCEMENTS:

February	IV./Zerstörergeschwader 1 (Bf-110)
March	Stab/Jagdgeschwader 3 (Bf-109G), I./Sturzkampfgeschwader 3 (Ju-87D), III/Kampfgeschwader 4 (He-111)
April	Fliegerkorps I, II., III./Jagdgeschwader 3 (Bf-109G), I., II./Jagdgeschwader 52 (Bf-109G); Stab, I., II., III./Sturzkampfgeschwader 2 (Ju-87D), III./Sturzkampfgeschwader 77 (Ju-87D); Stab, I., III./Kampfgeschwader 51 (Ju-88), Stab, I., II., III./Kampfgeschwader 55 (He-111), II./Schlachtgeschwader 1 (Fw-190A/Hs-123B)
May	79.Infanterie-Division
June	1st Mountain Division (Romanian)
July	98.Infanterie-Division, Romanian Armoured Battalion (T-38), Romanian 3rd Dive-Bombing Group (Ju-87D)

TRANSFERS:

26 February	46.Infanterie-Division begins transfer to Heeresgruppe Süd, but does not complete until late March.
26 February	198.Infanterie-Division begins transfer to Heeresgruppe Süd, but does not complete until April.
3 March	LII Armeekorps transferred to Heeresgruppe Süd.
17 March 1943	2nd Mountain Division (Romanian) to Crimea.
24 March	1.Gebirgs-Division to Greece.
May	5.Luftwaffen-Feld-Division to Crimea.
August	13.Panzer-Division to Heeresgruppe Süd.

SOVIET

TRANSCAUCASUS FRONT (ZAKAVKAZSKIY FRONTA – ZKF) (GENERAL IVAN V. TIULENEV)

Commissar: Lazar M. Kaganovich[5]
Black Sea Group of Forces (General Ivan E. Petrov)
18th Army (General-major Aleksandr I. Ryzhov)[6]
- 236th Rifle Division

---

1 Killed in action, 30 May 1943.
2 This unit was formerly the Sicherungs-Regiment 4 and included one squadron of Cossacks.
3 The third battalion lost all its rocket launchers in the retreat to the Kuban.
4 The Slovak Division was pulled out of the line on 1 February 1943 and was subsequently transferred to the Crimea. It only played a minor role in the opening days of the battle of Krasnodar.

5 Known as 'Iron Lazar', Kaganovich was a close associate of Stalin and a member of the Politburo. He was directly responsible for famines in the Ukraine, Crimea and Kuban in 1932–33 caused by his ruthless implementation of Stalin's forced collectivization policies. In 2010, Ukrainian courts ruled that Kaganovich was guilty of genocide against the Ukrainian people.
6 Ryzhov was replaced by General-major Konstantin A. Koroteev on 11 February, who was replaced by General-leytenant Konstantin N. Leselidze on 16 March 1943.

353rd Rifle Division
395th Rifle Division
10th, 68th and 119th Rifle brigades
40th Separate Motorized Rifle Brigade (General-major Nikita F. Tsepliaev)[7]
46th Army (General-major Ivan P. Roslyi)[8]
    9th Mountain Rifle Division
    31st Rifle Division
    2nd, 23rd, 33rd Mountain Rifle regiments
47th Army (General-leytenant Konstantin N. Leselidze)[9]
    3rd Rifle Corps[10]
        9th Rifle Brigade
        60th Rifle Brigade
        155th Rifle Brigade
    242nd Mountain Rifle Division
    176th Rifle Division
    216th Rifle Division
    318th Rifle Division
    337th Rifle Division
    339th Rifle Division
    383rd Rifle Division
    8th Guard Rifle Brigade
    103rd Rifle Brigade
    81st Naval Rifle Brigade
    255th Naval Rifle Brigade
    323rd Naval Rifle Battalion
    324th Naval Rifle Battalion
    327th Naval Rifle Battalion
    151st Tank Brigade
    62nd Independent Tank Battalion
    126th Independent Tank Battalion
    563rd Independent Tank Battalion
56th Army (General-major Andrei A. Grechko)
    10th Guards Rifle Corps (General-major Vasily V. Glagolev)[11]
        4th Guards Rifle Brigade
        5th Guards Rifle Brigade
        6th Guards Rifle Brigade
    32nd Guards Rifle Division
    55th Guards Rifle Division
    20th Mountain Rifle Division
    83rd Mountain Rifle Division
    61st Rifle Division
    394th Rifle Division
    9th Guards Rifle Brigade
    7th Rifle Brigade
    16th Rifle Brigade
    76th Rifle Brigade
    111st Rifle Brigade
    564th Independent Tank Battalion
5th Air Army (General-leytenant of Aviation Sergei K. Goriunov)
    286th Fighter Aviation Division (Isrebitelnyi Aviatsionnyi Division – IAD)
    165th Fighter Aviation Regiment (Isrebitelnyi Aviatsionnyi Polk – IAP) (La-5)
        171st Fighter Aviation Regiment (MiG-3)
        721st Fighter Aviation Regiment (LaGG-3)
        900th Fighter Aviation Regiment (Yak-1)
    295th Fighter Aviation Division
    116th Fighter Aviation Regiment

    164th Fighter Aviation Regiment (LaGG-3)
    502nd Ground Attack Aviation Regiment (Shturmovoy Aviatsionnyi Polk – ShAP) (Il-2)
    132nd Bomber Aviation Division (Bombardirovochnaya Aviatsionnaya Diviziya – BAD)
        63rd Bomber Aviation Regiment (Bombardirovochnyi Aviatsionnyi Polk – BAP) (Boston)
            367th Bomber Aviation Regiment (SB)
    718th Composite Aviation Regiment (Smeshannyi Aviatsionnyi Polk – SAP) (I-15/I-153)
    763rd Light Bomber Aviation Regiment (Legko Bombardirovochnyi Aviatsionnyi Polk – LBAP) (Po-2)
ZKF front-level forces:
    16th Rifle Corps
        51st Rifle Brigade
        107th Rifle Brigade
        165th Rifle Brigade
    328th Rifle Division
    402nd Rifle Division
    83rd Rifle Brigade
    31st Airborne Regiment[12]
    5th Guards Tank Brigade (Polkovnik Petr K. Shurenkov)[13]
    258th Independent Tank Battalion (Valentine/Lee)
    974th Bomber Aviation Regiment

North Caucasus Front (Severo-Kavkazskiy Front – CKF) (General-polkovnik Ivan I. Maslennikov)[14]
Commissar: General-major Aleksandr Ia. Fominykh
9th Army (General-major Konstantin A. Koroteev)[15]
    9th Rifle Corps
        43rd Rifle Brigade
        157th Rifle Brigade
        256th Rifle Brigade
    11th Guards Rifle Corps
        7th Guards Rifle Brigade
        8th Guards Rifle Brigade
        34th Rifle Brigade
        57th Rifle Brigade
    11th Rifle Corps (General-major Ivan A. Rubanyuk)
        12th Rifle Brigade
        84th Rifle Brigade
        131st Rifle Brigade
    207th Tank Brigade (T-26)
    562nd Independent Tank Battalion
37th Army (General-major Petr M. Kozlov)[16]
    2nd Guards Rifle Division
    223rd Rifle Division
    295th Rifle Division
    389th Rifle Division
    409th Rifle Division
    414th Rifle Division
58th Army (General-major Kondrat S. Mel'nik)
    77th Rifle Division
    276th Rifle Division
    317th Rifle Division
    351st Rifle Division
    417th Rifle Division
4th Air Army (General-major of Aviation Nikolai F. Naumenko)[17]
    217th Fighter Aviation Division
        84th Fighter Aviation Regiment (I-16)
        166 Fighter Aviation Regiment (LaGG-3)

---

7 This brigade was formed from the 72nd Cavalry Division and included a large number of Kuban Cossacks. It was provided with over 300 Lend-Lease vehicles to enhance its mobility.
8 Roslyi was replaced by General-major V. V. Glagolev in March 1943.
9 Leselidze took over 47th Army on 25 January 1943 and was replaced by General-major A. I. Ryzhov in March 1943. Ryzhov was replaced by General-major Petr M. Kozlov in July 1943.
10 This formation was known as the 3rd Mountain Rifle Corps until October 1942, then dropped the 'mountain' designation. In June 1943, it was redesignated as a Mountain unit and took command of the 9th, 83rd and 242nd Mountain Rifle divisions.
11 Replaced by General-major Ivan A. Rubaniuk on 12 February 1943.

12 This unit was formed by the Transcaucasus Front in January 1943 and consisted of two battalions with a total of 1,100 personnel.
13 The 5th GTB was one of the first Red Army units to field the American-built M4A2 Sherman tank. On 1 February 1943, the brigade had nine M4A2s, plus 20 M3 Lees and 18 Valentine tanks.
14 Maslennikov was replaced by General-leytenant Ivan E. Petrov in May 1943.
15 Koroteev was replaced by General-major Vasily V. Glagolev between February and March 1943, but returned in March. Grechkin took over the 9th Army in June 1943.
16 Replaced by General-leytenant Konstantin A. Koroteev in May 1943, who was replaced by General-major Aleksandr A. Filatov in July 1943.
17 Replaced by General-leytenant of Aviation Konstantin A. Vershinin in May 1943.

249 Fighter Aviation Regiment (LaGG-3)
40 Guards Fighter Aviation Regiment (La-5)
41st Guards Fighter Aviation Regiment (Gvardeiskyi
    Isrebitelnyi Aviatsionnyi Polk – GIAP) (La-5)
229th Fighter Aviation Division
    484th Fighter Aviation Regiment (Yak-1b)
    494th Fighter Aviation Regiment (MiG-3)[18]
219th Bomber Aviation Division (Pe-2)
216th Mixed Aviation Division
    16th Guards Fighter Aviation Regiment
    45th Fighter Aviation Regiment
    298th Fighter Aviation Regiment (P-39)
    66th Fighter Aviation Regiment (Yak-1)
    236th Bomber Aviation Regiment (Su-2)
230th Ground Attack Aviation Division (Shturmovoy
    Aviatsionnyi Division – ShAD)
    7th Guards Ground Attack Aviation Regiment (Gvardeiskyi
    Shturmovoy Aviatsionnyi Polk – GShAP)
        103rd Ground Attack Aviation Regiment (Il-2)
        210st Ground Attack Aviation Regiment (Il-2)
        590th Ground Attack Aviation Regiment (Il-2)
        926th Fighter Aviation Regiment (LaGG-3)
        446th Composite Aviation Regiment (Su-2/Po-2)
        750th Composite Aviation Regiment (Su-2/Po-2)
CKF front-level forces:
10th Rifle Corps
    89th Rifle Division
    59th Rifle Brigade
    62nd Rifle Brigade
    164th Rifle Brigade
4th Guards Cavalry Corps
    9th Guards Cavalry Division
    10th Guards Cavalry Division
    30th Cavalry Division
5th Guards Cavalry Corps
    11th Guards Cavalry Division
    12th Guards Cavalry Division
    63rd Cavalry Division
63rd Tank Brigade (T-34/Lee)
75th Independent Tank Battalion (Valentine)
132nd Independent Tank Battalion (Lee)
249th Independent Tank Battalion (Lee/Stuart)
Black Sea Fleet (Vice-Admiral Filipp Oktiabrskiy)[19]
Heavy cruiser *Voroshilov*
Light cruisers *Krasny Krym*, *Krasny Kavkaz*
Flotilla leader *Kharkov*
Destroyers *Boiky, Bezposhchadny, Soobrazitel'ny, Sposobnyi,
    Nezamozhnik, Zhelezniakov*
Minesweepers *T-403, T-404, T-407, T-411, T-412*
Gunboats *Krasny Adzharistan, Krasnaya Gruziya, Krasnaya
    Abkhaziya*[20]
1st Patrol Cutter Division
**Black Sea Fleet Naval Aviation Group (VVS-ChF) (General-major
Vasily V. Ermachenkov)**
4th Fighter Aviation Division–VMF (Voenno-Morskogo Flota –
    Military Maritime Fleet)
    25th Fighter Aviation Regiment–VMF (LaGG-3)
    62nd Fighter Aviation Regiment–VMF (LaGG-3/P-40E)
63rd Heavy Bomber Aviation Brigade–VMF
    40th Bomber Aviation Regiment–VMF (Pe-2)
    36th Mine-Torpedo Aviation Regiment–VMF (A-20C Boston)
    5th Guards Mine-Torpedo Aviation Regiment–VMF (Il-4)
11th Assault Aviation Brigade –VMF
    6th Guards Fighter Aviation Regiment–VMF

    9th Fighter Aviation Regiment–VMF (Yak-1)
    8th Guards Ground Attack Aviation Regiment
    47th Ground Attack Aviation Regiment (Il-2)
Azov Flotilla (Rear-Admiral Sergei Gorshkov)
Monitor *Zheleznyakov*
Patrol Boat *Kuban* (2 x 130mm, 3 x 45mm guns)
Medium landing craft – 3
Minesweepers – 6
KM-2/KM-4 patrol cutters – 18
Armoured cutters – 12
Reinforcements, February–September 1943:

February	45th Fighter Aviation Regiment, 298th Fighter Aviation Regiment (P-39D/K/N).
March	92nd Tank Brigade (Grant/Stuart), 257th Tank Regiment (Lee/Stuart).
April	3rd Fighter Aviation Corps (Isrebitelnyi Aviatsionnyi Korpus – IAK) (General-major Evgeniy I. Savitskiy) with 265th and 278th Fighter Aviation divisions (Yak-1b/Yak-7); 2nd Bomber Aviation Corps (Bombardirovochnaya Aviatsionnyi Korpus – BAK) (General-major Vladimir A. Ushakov) with 223rd and 285th Bomber Aviation divisions (Pe-2); 287th Fighter Aviation Division with 4th Fighter Aviation Regiment (Yak-7), 148th Fighter Aviation Regiment, 293rd Fighter Aviation Regiment (Yak-1); 2nd Composite Aviation Corps (General-major Ivan T. Eremenko) with 214th Ground Attack Aviation Division (Il-2), 201st Fighter Aviation Division (Yak-1/La-5) and 235th Fighter Aviation Division (La-5); 6th Long-Range Aviation Corps (Il-4 and Li-2VV).
May	57th Guards Fighter Aviation Regiment) (Spitfire Mk V), 1448th and 1449th Self-Propelled Artillery Regiments (Su-76/Su-122).
June	6th Guards Tank Regiment (KV-1), 85th and 258th Tank regiments (T-34/T-70), 244th and 257th Tank regiments (Lee/Stuart), 369th and 384th Separate Naval Infantry battalions (Otdelnyy Batalion Morskoy Pekhoty – OBMP).
August	494th Fighter Aviation Regiment (P-39).

---

18 The 494th IAP was re-equipped with P-39s in March 1943.
19 Only operational vessels are listed.
20 These three 1,400-ton ships were *Elpidifor*-type multi-purpose vessels, built in
    1920–23 as minesweepers, but heavily armed and capable of carrying up to 2,000
    troops each. They were armed with three 130mm guns and two 76mm guns, but
    little or no anti-aircraft defences. They could also carry field artillery and vehicles.

OPPOSING PLANS

AXIS

On 4 January 1943, the OKH directed 17.Armee to begin preparing a defensive position in the Kuban known as the Goten-Brückenkopfes or Gotenkopf (Goth's Head). Initial plans stated that both 17.Armee and 1.Panzerarmee would occupy the Gotenkopf, as well as large numbers of Luftwaffe personnel. The available construction troops, about ten battalions plus some Organization Todt personnel, were expected to create a defensive line that was hundreds of kilometres long by mid-March. About 5,600 local civilians were impressed to work on the project and some Soviet anti-tank ditches from the 1942 campaign were incorporated into the scheme, but it was a gargantuan task and rendered impossible by extended periods of rain and snow. Thus, German plans for the Gotenkopf were premised on the false assumption that defensive positions would be ready before the Soviets arrived in force in the region.

The man on the spot was Oberst Paul Betz, commander of the Pionier-Regiments-Stab 700 zbV, tasked with building the Gotenkopf out of virtual thin air, with limited resources and negligible time in the middle of winter. Since there were already some defences built to protect the area around Novorossiysk and Krymskaya, Betz decided to prioritize the area east of Krasnodar, where there were few defences. The critical sector was a 40km stretch between the fortified villages of Voronezhskaya and Korenoskaya, where Soviet armour was most likely to approach from the east. According to the orders for the construction of the Gotenkopf, the *Pioniere* were supposed to build numerous anti-tank ditches, machine-gun bunkers and field gun positions in this sector, but very little was completed before the Soviet 46th Army arrived.

The Axis logistical situation in the Kuban was sketchy from the start due to the loss of the rail link to Rostov. In early February, 17.Armee had over 320,000 troops and 100,000 horses, but there were no large logistic stockpiles in the Kuban; there was just enough food on hand for about two to three weeks. Fodder

A German infantry squad moves along a corduroy path through marshland. The terrain in the Kuban heavily favoured the defence and prevented the Red Army from bringing its numerical superiority to bear against 17.Armee. The grandiloquent title of Gothenkopf Stellung bestowed by Hitler upon the Kuban bridgehead made it sound like a fortress, rather than the muddy morass it actually was. (Nik Cornish at www.Stavka.org.uk)

for horses was in particularly short supply. Although about 30,000 'useless mouths' were soon sent to the Crimea to reduce logistical requirements, the margin remained narrow. Like 6.Armee at Stalingrad, 17.Armee in the Kuban would require an airlift to survive. However, the Luftwaffe's aerial resupply resources were gutted after the loss of 266 Ju-52 transports during the Stalingrad airlift. Most of the depleted transport groups were withdrawn to Germany to rebuild, leaving very little to support 17.Armee. Nevertheless, Luftflotte 4 directed Oberst Fritz Morzik to organize an airlift to support Ruoff's army. Morzik was a superb Lufttransportführer (air transport leader), who had organized the Demyansk and Stalingrad airlifts, but his remaining aircrews were exhausted and only a handful of transport planes were still operational. Thus, the Kuban airlift began as a shoestring effort.

Working from headquarters in Zaporozhe, Morzik pressed the Kampfgruppe zbV 200 with its 13 Fw-200C Condor aircraft into service as transports. (Kampfgruppe zbV 200 had already lost eight of its original 21 Fw-200Cs during the Stalingrad airlift.) The Condors had been taken from Kampfgeschwader 40 in France in order to support the Stalingrad airlift and were supposed to be returned to conduct their primary mission – long-range maritime reconnaissance for U-boats. Instead, beginning on 4 February, the Condors flew 76 sorties that delivered 242 tons of supplies and flew 1,887 troops out of the Kuban. On 14 February, the Condors were transferred back to France. Shortly thereafter, Morzik received two *Staffeln* with 22 Do-24 seaplanes and a *Staffel* of Ju-52/3m See floatplanes to support his airlift; these aircraft were able to deliver 100–200 tons per day in good weather, which was rare in February. By March, Luftflotte 4 was able to reorganize some of its Ju-52 transport groups, and operating from bases nearby in the Crimea, Morzik's airlift steadily increased its daily delivered tonnage. By mid-March, Morzik's transports reached their peak effort, flying in up to 600 tons in a single day.

Oberst Carl Henke, another *Pionier*, was put in charge of running logistic operations across the Kerch Strait, including organizing transport at the small ports and establishing a narrow-gauge railway from the Taman peninsula. The Kriegsmarine commander for the Black Sea, Vice-Admiral Robert Witthoeft-Emden, was ordered to concentrate shipping in Kerch to support 17.Armee. However, wintry weather in early January 1943 made crossing the 6-mile-wide Kerch Strait difficult and the Kriegsmarine was only able to deliver 800–900 tons of supplies by sea per day before Kerch harbour froze over on 14 January. Thereafter, there were virtually no supplies delivered by sea for the next three weeks. The 1. and 3.Landungsflotille based in Kerch had about 40 Marinefährprahm transports and four Siebel ferries available, but could not navigate the ice to the small port of Anapa until 7 February. (The Kriegsmarine had one small icebreaker at Kerch, which could not keep a sea lane open.) Thereafter, a trickle of seaborne supplies arrived and this expanded with the onset of warmer weather. Eventually, 70 per cent of all supplies to 17.Armee came by sea. Under decent weather conditions, a small convoy could traverse the distance from Kerch to Anapa in about six hours to deliver 500–600 tons of supplies.[21] However, 17.Armee, which was under constant attack, needed roughly 2,000 tons of supplies per day (food, ammunition, fuel) and the combined Luftwaffe/Kriegsmarine effort was only able to deliver the

21 The distance from Kerch to Anapa was 58 nautical miles. Some convoys originated from Feodosiya, which was a 75-nautical mile one-way trip.

bare minimum. Faced with this logistic limitation, on 7 March Hitler directed Organization Todt to begin building a 6km-long road and rail bridge across the Kerch Strait to support 17.Armee. Albert Speer, Reich Minister of Armaments, opposed the project as wasteful of resources, but bridge construction continued until the Kuban was evacuated. In the interim, German *Pionier* troops created a cable railway (*Drahtseilbahn*) over the Kerch Strait on 14 June 1943, which could deliver up to 1,000 tons per day across the waters.

German strategic plans for the Gotenkopf were driven by Hitler's obsession with maintaining the option to mount another offensive to seize the Caucasus oilfields in the summer of 1943, even though it was clear from the beginning that this would be logistically impossible. Yet when Hitler began considering where to conduct his next summer offensive, he never even considered the Kuban. Thus, the 'springboard for a future offensive' rationale was discarded by March 1943 and the real reason for the campaign was Hitler's grudging refusal to give up terrain.

The defence of the Kuban became Heeresgruppe A's primary task for most of 1943, with the main objective being simply to inflict maximum casualties on the enemy and tie down multiple Soviet armies. Thus, the Kuban was to be a battle of attrition. In reality, this strategy also deprived the Germans of over 200,000 troops who would have been better employed strengthening the southern front or creating a strategic reserve. As long as the Germans held the Kuban, the Soviets could not make a serious attempt to retake the Crimea. With a slim margin of reserves, 17.Armee could just hold the region, but the lines of communication to the Kuban were vulnerable to enemy air and sea interdiction, as well as bad weather. Yet if anything went seriously wrong, 17.Armee would find itself starving, like 6.Armee at Stalingrad.

Generalfeldmarschall Erich von Manstein, commander of Heeresgruppe Don (later Süd), was not happy with Hitler's decision to leave 17.Armee in the Kuban and constantly tried to siphon forces from this area to reinforce his own command. Although a trickle of replacements continued to arrive across the Kerch Strait to keep 17.Armee's defence intact, it was never enough, and the Red Army maintained the initiative throughout the campaign. Indeed, 17.Armee never had the strength to crush the Malaya Zemlya bridgehead or recover any lost terrain.

German troops loading a van onto a Pionierlandungsboot. Developed for Operation *Sea Lion*, the I-boat was assigned to special *Pionier* units and proved very handy for coastal traffic in both the Black and Baltic seas. The extended defence of the Kuban bridgehead was only possible due to the German ability to move adequate amounts of supplies across the Kerch Strait. (Nik Cornish at www.Stavka.org.uk)

A hard-bitten Soviet veteran soldier, winter 1942/43. After Stalingrad, for the first time in the war soldiers in the Red Army sensed that they were on the road to victory but many realized that they would not be around to see the final victory. Veterans such as this soldier had the ability to go toe-to-toe with the Germans, when their leadership put together a properly organized offensive. (Author's collection)

SOVIET

Operation *More* (*Sea*) and Operation *Gory* (*Mountains*) were the basis for initial Soviet offensive planning in the Kuban, which expected a fairly short campaign. It is not clear, but Stavka may have been surprised by the German refusal to evacuate 17.Armee from the Kuban, since these divisions were desperately needed in the Donbass region. It appears that Stavka believed that hasty offensives by Petrov and Maslennikov would seize enough territory to keep the Germans on the run and did not anticipate a protracted battle of attrition.

Yet when it became clear in February that the Germans intended to hold the Kuban, the pursuit ended and the North Caucasus Front had to shift gears to assemble the manpower, tanks, artillery and ammunition for a proper offensive. Up to that point, the multiple Soviet armies involved in the Kuban campaign had limited experience of working together since they had operated semi-independently during the previous Caucasus campaign. Nor were the constituent armies structured for combined-arms warfare; most rifle units had no tank support and fairly limited artillery support. Operating in mountainous terrain, most of the Soviet units had only light artillery and few vehicles. When it was clear that Maslennikov and Petrov had difficulty coordinating their operations, Stavka sent Marshal Zhukov to serve as a front-level supervisor, although he played a major role in developing plans for the first major offensive against the Gotenkopf.

Up to this point in the war, the Red Army had not demonstrated much skill in breaking through German fortified lines, even weak ones. Instead, when faced with stout resistance, Red Army commanders tried to bludgeon their way through the German *Hauptkampflinie* (HKL, main line of resistance), leading to heavy casualties – which is exactly what the Germans hoped to achieve. In the Kuban, the Red Army would begin to experiment with new tactical methods to get around fortified lines, but with only limited success.

Yet there was no need to fight a battle of attrition on German terms since supply was the Achilles heel of the Gotenkopf. If German logistics across the Kerch Strait were disrupted, 17.Armee could not hold the Kuban. However, Stavka was slow to recognize the vulnerability of 17.Armee to a coordinated air–sea interdiction campaign because it was dominated by soldiers and Stalin had little interest in naval affairs. Soviet doctrine held that the navy and air force were supposed to support army operations, not the other way around. While the VVS-ChF did conduct regular air attacks against the ports of Kerch and Anapa, these inflicted only modest damage. Soviet aircraft even managed to sink some German naval transports in the Kerch Strait and naval mines damaged a few more, but the effort devoted to the interdiction campaign was grossly insufficient. Likewise, the Black Sea Fleet had a considerable superiority in surface warships, light craft and submarines, which consistently failed to accomplish much. The Soviet failure to interdict German supply lines across the Kerch Strait was clearly a result of the lack of joint doctrine between the Red Army, the Black Sea Fleet and VVS; no joint campaign plan was ever developed.

THE CAMPAIGN

17.ARMEE WITHDRAWS TO THE KUBAN BRIDGEHEAD, FEBRUARY 1943

As February 1943 began, Stalin was dissatisfied with the inability of Petrov's forces to break through to Krasnodar and the slow progress of Operation *Gory*. Through Stavka, he directed that Petrov's forces, with a little help from Maslennikov's North Caucasus Front, were to take both Novorossiysk and Krasnodar by mid-February. Consequently, Petrov was forced to adopt high-risk methods – which he was uncomfortable with – in order to accomplish these missions.

Amphibious landings, 4 February

Since early January, Stalin had been pressing for the Black Sea Fleet to mount an amphibious invasion south of Novorossiysk to outflank 17.Armee and cut it off from its route of retreat into the Taman Peninsula. Both the army and the fleet leadership were unenthusiastic, given their previous misadventures with amphibious operations in the Crimea, but began assembling troops and shipping in the ports of Batumi and Gelendzhik. Petrov included the amphibious operation in his planning for Operation *More*, but did not want to conduct the landing until the 47th Army achieved some kind of success in its ground offensive. When success on the ground proved elusive, Stalin ordered Petrov to conduct the landing as soon as possible, believing that it would unhinge the German defence.

Vice-Admiral Filipp S. Oktiabrskiy, commander of the Black Sea Fleet, formed a bombardment group under his command, consisting of the cruisers *Voroshilov*, *Krasny Krym* and *Krasny Kavkaz*, the flotilla leader *Kharkov* and three destroyers – virtually all his remaining operational surface units. Rear-Admiral Nikolai E. Basisty was put in charge of the landing group, which consisted of three 1,400-ton *Elpidifor*-type landing ships, three tank transport barges, five minesweepers and a

The cruiser *Voroshilov*, commissioned in June 1940, was the largest operational unit in the Black Sea Fleet in February 1943. The *Voroshilov* supported the amphibious landings near Novorossiysk with her nine 180mm guns. However, she had been damaged previously by German mines and bombers, and the Black Sea Fleet was reluctant to expose its few remaining major surface warships for long in contested areas. (Author's collection)

Opening moves, 4–27 February 1943

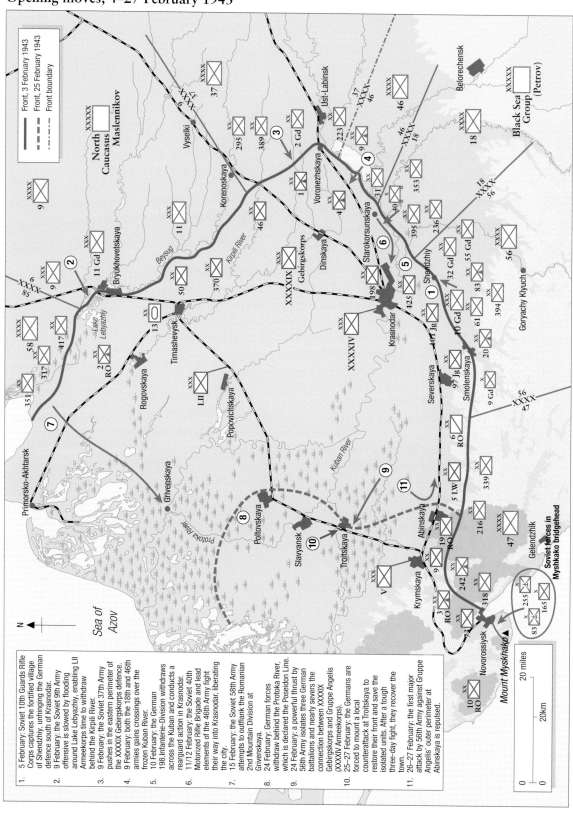

1. 5 February: Soviet 10th Guards Rifle Corps captures the fortified village of Shendzhiy, unhinging the German defence south of Krasnodar.
2. 9 February: the Soviet 9th Army offensive is slowed by flooding around Lake Lebyazhiy, enabling LII Armeekorps to withdraw behind the Kirpili River.
3. 9 February: the Soviet 37th Army pushes in the eastern perimeter of the XXXXIX Gebirgskorps defence.
4. 9 February: both the 18th and 46th armies gains crossings over the frozen Kuban River.
5. 10 February: the German 198.Infanterie-Division withdraws across the Kuban and conducts a rearguard action in Krasnodar.
6. 11/12 February: the Soviet 40th Motorized Rifle Brigade and lead elements of the 46th Army fight their way into Krasnodar, liberating the city.
7. 15 February: the Soviet 58th Army attempts to outflank the Romanian 2nd Mountain Division at Grivenskaya.
8. 24 February: German forces withdraw behind the Protoka River, which is declared the Poseidon Line.
9. 24 February: a powerful thrust by 56th Army isolates three German battalions and nearly severs the connection between XXXXIX Gebirgskorps and Gruppe Angelis (XXXIV Armeekorps).
10. 25–27 February: the Germans are forced to mount a local counterattack at Troitskaya to restore their front and save the isolated units. After a tough three-day fight, they recover the town.
11. 26–27 February: the first major attack by 56th Army against Gruppe Angelis' outer perimeter at Abinskaya is repulsed.

The *Krasnaya Abkhaziya* was one of the *Elpidifor*-type vessels that landed Soviet naval infantry near Novorossiysk on 4 February 1943. These vessels were an odd combination of heavily armed minesweeper and cargo ship, equipped with three 130mm guns and a variety of lighter armament. Each could carry a naval infantry battalion, crammed on deck, and some vehicles. The Soviet Navy did not build purpose-designed amphibious craft in World War II, but instead employed a wide variety of vessels. (Author's collection)

flotilla of patrol boats. The first echelon of the invasion force would consist of Polkovnik Aleksei S. Potapov's 255th Naval Rifle Brigade and the second echelon consisted of the 83rd Naval Rifle Brigade. Petrov provided another rifle brigade and an anti-tank unit as follow-on forces. Altogether, Petrov and Oktiabrskiy committed about 10,000 troops to the landing operation. The Black Sea Fleet had also created a commando-type unit, the 305th Naval Infantry Battalion under Major Caesar L. Kunikov, which Oktiabrskiy wanted to use as a diversionary force.

The primary target chosen for the landing was Ozereyka Bay, about 8km south-west of Novorossiysk. Ozereyka Bay was not a very good choice, due to its narrow, pebble-covered beach overlooked by steep cliffs, but it was not expected to be heavily defended. Actual intelligence on enemy dispositions was negligible. Oktiabrskiy decided that Major Kunikov's battalion would stage a diversionary landing across Tsemes Bay, to attack enemy coastal batteries near Stanichka. It was true that Generalleutnant Rudolf von Bünau's 73.Infanterie-Division only had about one-third of its strength holding Novorossiysk and had detachments spread out all along the coast, stretching back to Anapa. The Romanian 10th Infantry Division was also defending positions along the coast, including an infantry company and a 120mm mortar battery at Ozereyka Bay. Yet unknown to Oktiabrskiy, Heeres-Küsten-Artillerie-Abteilung 789, which had three batteries of Czech-made 10.5cm K35(t) cannons and one battery of 10.5cm lFH18 howitzers, overlooked the beach. Unlike much captured artillery in German service, the Skoda K35 was a modern weapon with a high rate of fire.

Although the Germans were not expecting an amphibious landing during the rainy first week of February, Oktiabrskiy imprudently used his surface action group to bombard German positions in the Novorossiysk area on the night of 30/31 January,

A German 10.5cm lFH18 light howitzer firing. This was the standard German divisional artillery piece in World War II. Note the soldiers are wearing mosquito netting on their helmets, since the marshy Kuban was conducive to certain strains of malaria. (Nik Cornish at www.Stavka.org.uk)

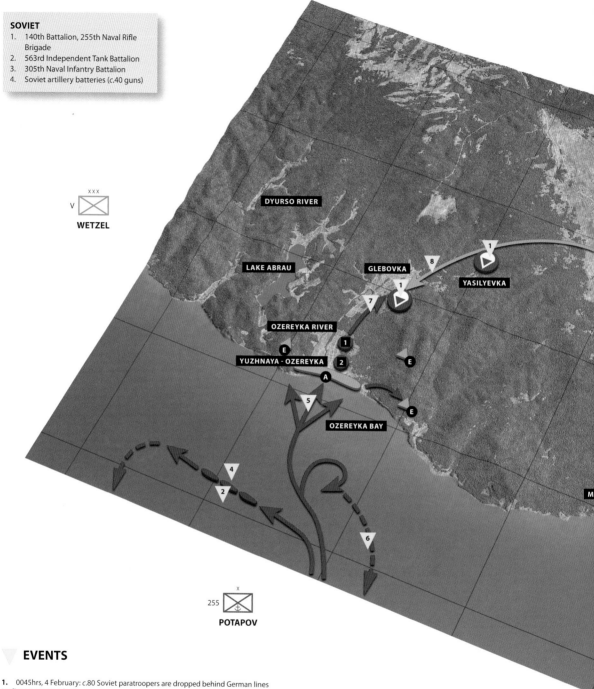

SOVIET

1. 140th Battalion, 255th Naval Rifle Brigade
2. 563rd Independent Tank Battalion
3. 305th Naval Infantry Battalion
4. Soviet artillery batteries (c.40 guns)

WETZEL

DYURSO RIVER

LAKE ABRAU

GLEBOVKA

YASILYEVKA

OZEREYKA RIVER

YUZHNAYA - OZEREYKA

OZEREYKA BAY

POTAPOV

EVENTS

1. 0045hrs, 4 February: *c.*80 Soviet paratroopers are dropped behind German lines to disrupt communications.

2. 0100hrs, 4 February: the Soviet Black Sea Fleet surface action group arrives off Ozereyka Bay but decides to delay the bombardment to await the transports. One destroyer which did not receive this message opens fire, alerting the Axis coastal defences.

3. 0111hrs, 4 February: Major Kunikov's 305th Naval Infantry Battalion lands virtually unopposed near Stanichka and is reinforced before dawn. Kunikov fortifies his small beachhead.

4. 0230hrs, 4 February: the Soviet squadron begins a 35-minute naval bombardment of the enemy defences at Ozereyka Bay.

5. 0335hrs, 4 February: a reinforced battalion-size assault detachment from the 255th Naval Rifle Brigade begins its landing at Ozereyka Bay, but suffers heavy losses. The main body of transports waits offshore.

6. 0620hrs, 4 February: after assessing the main landing as a failure, the Soviet fleet withdraws back to port.

7. Morning, 4 February: the Soviet landing force pushes inland to Glebovka, overrunning a few enemy positions, but is leaderless and without supplies.

8. Afternoon, 4 February: a battalion from 101.Jäger-Division and some troops from 4.Gebirgs-Division are hurriedly moved by truck to eliminate the Soviet troops around Glebovka.

9. 1725hrs, 4 February: the first small-scale German counterattacks against Major Kunikov's beachhead begin.

Note: Gridlines are shown at intervals of 5 km (3.1 miles)

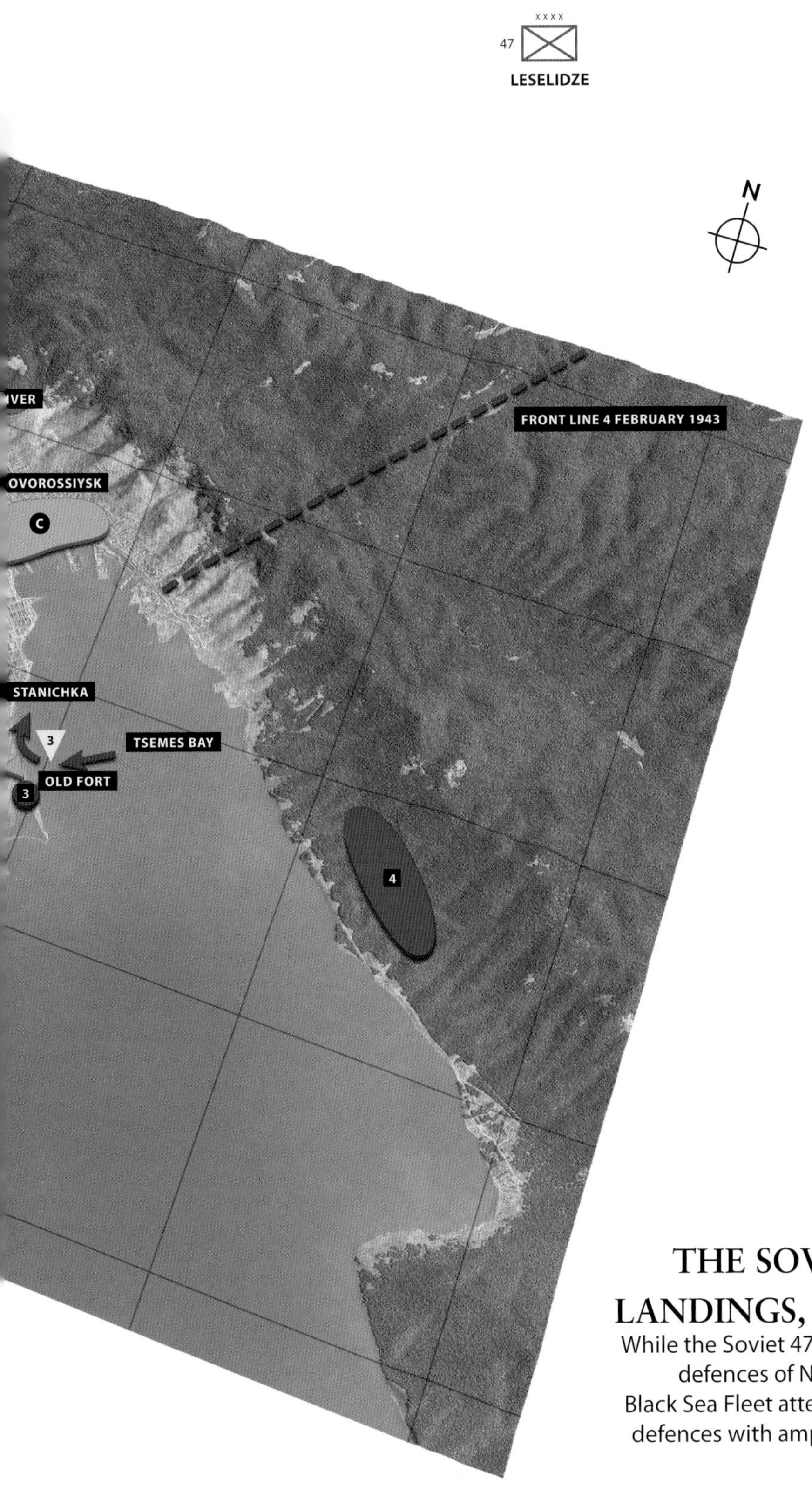

XXXX
47 ⊠
LESELIDZE

GERMAN/ROMANIAN
A. 5th Company, 38th Infantry
    Regiment, 10th Infantry
    Regiment, 10th Infantry Division
    (Romanian)
B. Kampfgruppe Krauss (III./Jäger-
    Regiment 229 from 101.Jäger-
    Division)
C. Grenadier-Regiment 186 (73.
    Infanterie-Division)
D. Kampfgruppe Wolf (2 platoons
    of *Pioniere* and one Panzerjäger
    Kompanie)
E. German coastal battery

N

FRONT LINE 4 FEBRUARY 1943

IVER

OVOROSSIYSK

C

XX
73 ⊠
VON BÜNAU

STANICHKA

3   **TSEMES BAY**

OLD FORT

3

4

THE SOVIET AMPHIBIOUS
LANDINGS, 4 FEBRUARY 1943

While the Soviet 47th Army attacked the German
defences of Novorossiysk from the east, the
Black Sea Fleet attempted to outflank the enemy
defences with amphibious landings at Ozereyka
Bay and Stanichka.

followed by a diversionary attack with destroyers on the port of Anapa. These actions only served to put the Germans on alert that the Black Sea Fleet was up to something and all coastal defences were put on high alert. On the afternoon of 3 February, the amphibious forces began assembling and left their ports, but well behind schedule. Communications between the bombardment group and the landing group were intermittent and Oktiabrskiy was not aware that Basisty's landing force was running late.

The operation began at 0045hrs on 4 February with 57 paratroopers from the 31st Airborne Regiment jumping near the villages of Vasilyevka and Glebovka; their mission was to disrupt enemy communications near the landing beaches. By luck, the Germans managed to kill the lieutenant in charge of this detachment when he landed, depriving the unit of leadership. While the paratroops did manage to harass some enemy artillery batteries, all but two were lost in the operation.

Oktiabrskiy had intended to begin his naval bombardment at 0100hrs, but when he realized that Basisty's landing force had not yet arrived, he decided to delay. Yet in war, there is always someone who does not get the word and the destroyer *Boikiy* opened fire anyway, alerting the Germans. Meanwhile, 9km to the east, Major Kunikov's battalion was crossing Tsemes Bay on seven small boats from the 4th Patrol Division, commanded by Leytenant Nikolai Sipiagin. Just before they reached the opposite shore, Soviet artillery south of Novorossiysk opened fire on the coast. Although there was a German coastal battery with two 8.8cm Flak guns emplaced near Stanichka, it somehow did not notice Sipiagin's small flotilla approaching. It is also important to remember that in war, luck can be a determining factor. At 0111hrs, the Soviet craft reached the shore and Kunikov rapidly disembarked with 250 of his men. Sipiagin turned around and went back for the rest of the battalion, while Kunikov's troops stealthily moved into a nearby school and waited. The nearby Axis troops responded with only light harassing fire in the darkness, killing one of Kunikov's sailors and wounding three, then abandoned the Flak position.

With the night quickly passing, Oktiabrskiy decided to begin his bombardment at 0230hrs, even though the landing force was still not quite ready. The Soviet warships fired 2,292 medium-calibre rounds at the beach area but in the darkness without any kind of observation, little was accomplished. There was no response from the enemy and the beach area remained quiet. Oktiabrskiy's bombardment ended at 0305hrs but Basisty's landing force did not begin moving towards the shore for another 30 minutes. Finally, Basisty sent in his assault echelon, consisting of 300 naval infantrymen from the 140th Battalion, 255th Naval Infantry Battalion crowded into six MO-IV-type patrol boats and the three barges carrying the 30 Stuart light tanks of the 563rd Independent Tank Battalion and another 1,200 troops. On the way in, the cutter *SKA-051* struck a mine and exploded, killing the commander of the assault echelon. Now the German defences came alive, with a searchlight illuminating the

Major Caesar L. Kunikov, commander of the 305th Naval Infantry Battalion, which succeeded in creating the Malaya Zemlya (Little Land) beachhead. The 33-year-old Kunikov came from a Russian-Jewish family in Rostov and had joined the Azov Flotilla in 1941. His seizure of the Malaya Zemlya beachhead was a critical success for the Soviets. However, Kunikov was badly wounded in the defence of the beachhead and died on 13 February 1943. He was posthumously awarded the Hero of the Soviet Union. (Author's collection)

Ozereyka Bay, where the Soviet Black Sea Fleet made an amphibious landing before dawn on 4 February 1943. The German artillery batteries were on the high ground, overlooking the bay. (Author's collection)

beach. The guns of Heeres-Küsten-Artillerie-Abteilung 789 opened fire and scored multiple hits on the Soviet craft, including one of the barges. About 1,400 troops managed to scramble ashore, but only 12 of the 30 Stuart tanks were disembarked. The German artillery shot the wallowing assault craft to pieces and when Basisty tried to send in more vessels, they were repulsed. By 0620hrs, the sun was up and Basisty ordered the landing force to retire before the Luftwaffe arrived. The landing force was left to its fate.

On shore, small groups of naval infantry and a few Stuart tanks pushed inland, overrunning some Axis gun positions; Heeres-Küsten-Artillerie-Abteilung 789 lost some of its artillery and suffered eight dead and nine wounded. By midday, some troops had reached their objective, the village of Glebovka, but they were desperately short of ammunition and had no communications with the Black Sea Fleet. Six Stuart tanks that made it inland were quickly knocked out. No real perimeter was ever established. Initially, the German reaction to the landings was restrained, since V Armeekorps was uncertain how large a force had landed in Ozereyka Bay and Kunikov's landing at Stanichka was regarded as a feint. Von Bünau's 73.Infanterie-Division sent its quick reaction force – Panzerjäger-Abteilung 173 and a few alarm companies – to Ozereyka Bay and 101.Jäger-Division sent a battalion (Gruppe Krauss) from Krymskaya by truck. Without leadership or supplies, the Soviet troops were quickly eliminated. By the end of the day, the landing force had been crushed, with the Germans counting 620 dead and 594 prisoners. About 100 naval infantrymen tried to reach Kunikov's beachhead, but their fate is unknown.

Both von Bünau and General der Infanterie Wilhelm Wetzel, commander of V Armeekorps, were satisfied that the Soviet landing in Ozereyka Bay was destroyed but

German Gebirgsjäger survey Soviet wreckage in Ozereyka Bay, 6 February 1943. In the foreground, a German 10.5cm howitzer with shattered barrel lies near the wreck of a Soviet landing barge and a destroyed M3 Stuart light tank. The Soviet landing craft were literally shot to pieces by the German gun positions. Although several German gun positions like this one were overrun by naval infantrymen, the landing had already suffered grievous losses. Note the narrow, stony beach, which channelled the attackers right into the German defences. (Author's collection)

MAJOR KUNIKOV'S DEFENCE OF HIS BEACHHEAD, 5 FEBRUARY 1943 (PP. 34–35)

As part of their opening move to liberate the Kuban region, the Soviets decided to mount a major amphibious operation to capture Novorossiysk from the south. Although the main landing at Ozereyka Bay was a fiasco, a smaller landing at Stanichka by Major Caesar Kunikov's 305th Naval Infantry Battalion succeeded in gaining a toehold on the morning of 4 February. Kunikov had barely 800 lightly equipped troops, and their original mission had simply been to draw enemy attention away from the main landing. However, after that failed, Kunikov decided to dig in around a brick schoolhouse on the southern side of Stanickha and wait for reinforcements. After some tentative probes in the late afternoon of 4 February, Kampfgruppe Wolf, comprised of *Pioniere* and Panzerjäger from 73.Infanterie-Division, began a series of counterattacks on the morning of 5 February, trying to determine where Kunikov's positions were in order to eliminate them. This was one of the defining moments of the Kuban campaign, where the bravery of Kunikov's determined troops shaped the eventual outcome.

Initially, the German counterattacks were just platoon-size efforts, supported by a few vehicles, as shown in this illustration. Here, Kunikov (**1**) has caught an enemy infantry squad (**2**) in the open, along with a StuG III assault gun (**3**). Many of the German infantry are hit and the StuG III will soon withdraw after being hit several times by anti-tank rifle fire, such as from the PTRD-41 rifle shown (**4**).

During the course of the day, a dozen German counterattacks were repulsed. Kunikov's troops ran short of ammunition and eventually had to abandon their position in the school, but they grimly formed a new perimeter near the water's edge. Kunikov's situation was desperate, but the Germans lacked sufficient troops and decided to defer an all-out assault until more reinforcements arrived. Late on 5 February, the Soviet Black Sea Fleet began landing 5,000 troops who had been destined for the Ozereyka Bay landing, but were now diverted to Stanichka. By the time that the Germans renewed their attacks, the Soviet beachhead had been heavily reinforced.

During the rest of February, the Soviets continued to pour more troops into the beachhead, which expanded to include Mount Myskhako and was dubbed Malaya Zemlya (Little Land). Although Kunikov later died defending the beachhead, the creation of this lodgement south of Novorossiysk seriously complicated the German defence of the Kuban.

The scene at Ozereyka Bay on the morning of 5 February 1943 after the disastrous Soviet landing attempt. About 12 M3 Stuart light tanks made it ashore with over 1,000 troops in the first wave, but the landing craft were badly shot up by German artillery and the follow-on waves turned back. Without supplies, the beachhead was quickly overwhelmed. (Author's collection)

apparently thought Kunikov's force was only a small raiding party. Initially, the only force sent to deal with Kunikov was Gruppe Wolf, consisting of two engineer platoons from Pionier-Bataillon 173 under a Hauptmann Karl Wolf. It was not until 0900hrs that Wolf's *Pioniere* encountered Kunikov's troops and they were quickly halted by heavy small arms fire, as well as artillery barrages from across the bay. After the Ozereyka Bay area was mopped up, Gruppe Krauss was sent to Stanichka, along with alarm units that included signal troops and Kriegsmarine personnel.

The next day, the Germans mounted a dozen small attacks on Kunikov's position, supported by a handful of assault guns, but failed to overrun the tough defenders. In fact, the German attackers were outnumbered by 2:1. Wetzel immediately asked 17.Armee for reinforcements and 13.Panzer-Division dispatched Gruppe Lehmann (I./Panzergrenadier-Regiment 93) and 198.Infanterie-Division sent the entire Grenadier-Regiment 305. However, it would take time for these reinforcements to arrive and Kunikov was given a brief reprieve. Nevertheless, Kunikov's troops were virtually out of ammunition and could not survive another day without supplies. Oktiabrskiy apparently wrote off both beachheads but after he returned to port, a radio report from Kunikov was received and Oktiabrskiy was ordered to drop the main landing force into the Stanichka beachhead.[22] At 2230hrs on 5 February, two *Elpidifor*-type ships arrived at Stanichka to offload the remainder of Potapov's 255th Naval Rifle Battalion and the 165th Rifle Brigade. On the night of 6/7 February, the 31st Airborne Regiment was landed as well. By the morning of 7 February, there were over 8,000 Soviet troops in the Malaya Zemlya (Little Land) beachhead, while the Germans had only

A Luftwaffe aerial image, taken in 1941, showing the area where Major Kunikov's naval infantry battalion landed south of Novorossiysk in February 1943. Kunikov's initial landing occurred near the Old Fort (C), where the Germans stationed two 8.8cm guns. A radio station (B) was also located next to the Old Fort. Major Kunikov's troops occupied a few buildings in the strip extending from the suburb of Stanichka, in the top part of the image. (Author's collection)

22 Oktiabrskiy's poor performance in this amphibious operation contributed to him being relieved of command several months later.

The Soviet MO-IV type patrol boats were used to land troops in the Malaya Zemlya beachhead and proved handy throughout the campaign, although they were no match for the faster German S-boats. The 50-ton MO-IV class carried a 45mm cannon and two 12.7mm heavy machine guns, with a crew of up to 20 men. (Author's collection)

been able to throw a thin screen of fewer than 2,000 troops around them.

Wetzel and von Bünau did not mount a serious counterattack against the Malaya Zemlya beachhead until the morning of 7 February and this effort comprised just three incomplete battalion-size *Kampfgruppen*. The attack was a complete failure. By the time that the Germans brought up more troops and some heavy artillery on 9 February, the Soviets had crammed over 10,000 troops into the small beachhead and were dug in. Armed with this massive superiority in numbers, the Soviets pushed south out of the beachhead, overrunning the screen of Romanian cavalrymen deployed to the south, and occupied Mount Myskhako. Once the Soviets controlled this high ground, their lodgement could not be eliminated with anything less than a corps-size attack.

The battle for Krasnodar and retreat, 9–27 February

By 1 February, General der Artillerie Maximilian de Angelis' XXXXIV Armeekorps (known as Gruppe Angelis) had erected a firm defence to the south of Krasnodar with 125. and 198.Infanterie-Division and 101.Jäger-Division, which effectively blocked Grechko's 56th Army. Generalmajor Emil Vogel's 101.Jäger-Division had established a particularly strong defensive position with Kampfgruppe Schury (three infantry battalions) south of Krasnodar in the town of Shendzhiy. The eastern approaches to Krasnodar were covered by General der Gebirgstruppe Rudolf Konrad's XXXXIX Gebirgskorps with 1. and 4.Gebirgs-Division and the 46.Infanterie-Division.

The German XXXXIX Gebirgskorps was forced to build a number of outposts in the marshy lagoon area but due to the high water table they could not dig in. Instead, timber-faced positions provided a small measure of protection against enemy infantry weapons. These positions were constantly under attack by Soviet infiltrators and enemy aircraft. (Nik Cornish at www. Stavka.org.uk)

Betz's construction troops had not yet completed much in the way of obstacles or prepared positions in this sector, so Konrad's troops were forced to hold hasty field positions. The departure of the Slovak Mobile Division, which had just been pulled out of the line in order to withdraw it from the Kuban, left the Germans without any appreciable reserve in this sector.

On the same day as the landing at Ozereyka Bay, Petrov issued orders to his 18th, 46th and 56th armies to prepare for a converging attack upon Krasnodar, from the east and the south. Maslennikov's 9th and 37th armies would support this effort by attacking from the east. However, Petrov had great difficulty organizing this hasty offensive, since much of his artillery was still moving to the front and his supplies were inadequate. Rainy weather slowed everything to a crawl. According to Grechko's post-war history, the Soviets needed to employ one-third of their available manpower just to repair roads and bridges. Nevertheless, on 9 February, Petrov and Maslennikov began their offensives. Right away, the 9th Army ran into serious difficulty from flooding around Lake Lebyazhny and the Beysug River, which allowed LII Armeekorps to withdraw unmolested behind the Kirpili River at Timashevsk. The 13.Panzer-Division was deployed to anchor the new line on that city. General-major Petr M. Kozlov's 37th Army had more luck, overrunning the intended Gotenkopf strongholds in Voronezhskaya and Korenoskaya before 1. and 4.Gebirgs-Division could establish a viable HKL. As Kozlov advanced, Konrad's corps began withdrawing westwards. Heavy rains were a nuisance but did not halt the Soviet advance.

South of the Kuban River, General-major Ivan P. Roslyi's 46th Army – which only had two rifle divisions – attacked across the river and achieved a bridgehead. General-major Aleksandr I. Ryzhov, commander of the 18th Army, also noticed that Konrad's corps had pulled back from the Kuban River and he immediately sent infantry to gain a crossing, then had his engineers construct a pontoon bridge. Once the bridge was completed, he brought up General-major Nikita F. Tsepliaev's 40th Separate Motorized Rifle Brigade, his only motorized formation, and sent them across. Tsepliaev's brigade included a large number of Kuban Cossacks and they rode into battle on US-built Dodge trucks. The 4.Gebirgs-Division tried to establish a strongpoint at Starokunskaya on the Kuban River, but with the flank units retreating, this position was abandoned without a fight. Meanwhile, Grechko's 56th Army had eliminated 101. Jäger-Division's strongpoint at Shendzhiy and Gruppe Angelis began withdrawing north to Krasnodar. On the morning of 10 February, German rearguards from 198.Infanterie-Division crossed the Kuban into Krasnodar and blew up the last bridges.

Gruppe Angelis did not mount a serious effort to defend Krasnodar but

A current monument in the Malaya Zemlya beachhead at the site of Major Kunikov's landing near Stanickha. It is apparent that the short distance across Tsemes Bay could be crossed by small craft in a short time even at night. The landing force received artillery support from guns positioned on the far side of Tsemes Bay. (Author's collection)

Cossacks serving with the Red Army in the Kuban. Most of the North Caucasus Front's cavalry went toward Rostov, but some smaller cavalry detachments supported the advance into the Kuban. In particular, General-major Tsepliaev's 40th Separate Motorized Rifle Brigade included a large number of Kuban Cossacks. (Author's collection)

instead conducted a delaying operation with 198.Infanterie-Division. The Grenadier-Regiment 326 tried to delay Tsepliaev's brigade in the south-east suburbs of Krasnodar, but Soviet troops began entering the outskirts on the afternoon of 11 February and overran the Luftwaffe airfield. Gruppe Angelis fought just long enough to allow an orderly evacuation of the city while *Pioniere* blew up infrastructure, including an oil refinery. Before dawn on 12 February, Tsepliaev's brigade advanced to the main train station with a single battalion and found negligible resistance. Soon, troops from the 18th Army also advanced into the city.

In the north, XXXXIX Gebirgskorps and LII Armeekorps pulled back further, abandoning Timashevsk. During the retreat of 46.Infanterie-Division, Generalmajor Haccius was shot and killed on 11 February. It was already apparent to the OKH that 17.Armee lacked the strength to hold the original position sketched out for the Gotenkopf and new rearward phase lines were quickly established. Once Krasnodar was liberated, Stavka hoped to crush a good portion of the retreating 17.Armee with a pincer attack by Petrov's and Maslennikov's forces, but this proved beyond their capabilities at the moment. Over the next 12 days, 17.Armee conducted a series of phased withdrawals which kept it just ahead of the converging enemy armies. On 15 February, General-major Kondrat S. Mel'nik's 58th Army pushed hard against the retreating Romanian 2nd Mountain Division, trying to get around their open flank near Grivenskaya with two rifle divisions. Since the Axis had almost no troops in this frozen, marshy area, LII Armeekorps' left flank was exposed. The 13.Panzer-Division quickly dispatched Kampfgruppe Hake with its available armour to prevent the Romanian division from being overwhelmed. Nevertheless, 58th Army kept sending troops deeper into the marshland, where Panzers could not go. The 17.Armee was forced to conduct a fighting retreat, turning every so often to fend off its pursuers. Although the pursuing Soviet armies and the VVS repeatedly attacked the retreating German columns, they failed to destroy any units and Axis losses were light. In two weeks, XXXXIX Gebirgskorps suffered fewer than 200 dead and missing. By 24 February, LII Armeekorps and XXXXIX Gebirgskorps had successfully withdrawn behind the Protoka River, which was dubbed the Poseidon Line, while Gruppe Angelis took over the defence of the Krymskaya sector.

During the same period, Gruppe Angelis fought a desperate battle against Grechko's 56th Army, retreating from Severskaya to Krymskaya. On 24 February, a battalion of Soviet tanks cut off Kampfgruppe Schury ten miles east of Krymskaya, and 1.Gebirgs-Division was forced to mount a hasty counterattack to rescue this force. A three-day battle for the town of Troitskaya resulted in a German tactical victory that restored their front line and enabled Kampfgruppe Schury to withdraw intact.

A young German soldier in a trench in the Kuban. The German infantrymen in the Kuban were forced to fight a static battle of attrition around strongpoints like Krymskaya which were reminiscent of World War I battles. Although 17.Armee managed to repulse all the Soviet offensives directed against it, the troops required to hold the useless Kuban bridgehead were badly needed elsewhere on the Eastern Front. (Author's collection)

Stand on the Poseidon Line, 25 February–31 March

By 25 February, 17.Armee had withdrawn into a much more compact perimeter, with its 12 German and four Romanian divisions holding a front line that was about 120km long. Nevertheless, Ruoff only had two battalions in reserve, including one from Generalmajor Wilhelm Crisolli's threadbare 13.Panzer-Division, to guard against a Soviet amphibious landing on the Taman Peninsula. The main focus of the German defence was centred on the town of Krymskaya, held by Generalleutnant Ernst Rupp's 97.Jäger-Division. Rupp's division established an advanced position at Abinskaya, 12km east of Krymskaya, with Kampfgruppe Otte. Oberst Friedrich-Wilhelm Otte, commander of Jäger-Regiment 207, only had three infantry battalions in Abinskaya, but he was supported by two Nebelwerfer batteries, 40 medium artillery pieces and a 2cm Flak battery. Rupp's intent was for Otte to delay the Soviet advance westwards along the railway in order to gain time for German engineers to fortify Krymskaya. Grechko's 56th Army began

A German machine-gun position covers a likely enemy avenue of approach in the Lagoon sector. Unlike the Krymskaya sector, most combat in the Lagoon sector occurred at very close quarters. This also proved a very unhealthy area, since it was infested by mosquitos that spread malaria. (Süddeutsche Zeitung, 00404131)

probing the Abinskaya sector almost immediately and launched a serious attack on 26–27 February, which Otte repulsed. On 10 March, Grechko attacked Kampfgruppe Otte's positions at Abinskaya again, but was repulsed after four days of heavy fighting. Kampfgruppe Otte finally evacuated the Abinskaya position on 24 March, having accomplished its mission.

North of the Kuban River, repeated efforts by the Soviet 9th and 37th armies to penetrate the front of the German line held by Ott's LII Armeekorps and Konrad's XXXXIX Gebirgskorps along the Protoka were repulsed. The 1.Gebirgs-Division anchored the northern sector at the town of Slavyansk. In late February, General-major Kondrat S. Mel'nik's 58th Army began turning the LII Armeekorps' left flank by sending two of its rifle divisions (317 and 361) through the marshes bordering the Sea of Azov. This area – referred to as 'the Lagoon' by the Germans – was extremely flat and waterlogged, with no roads, but ideal for infiltration by light infantry. Mel'nik put his deputy General-major Mikhail S. Filippovsky in charge of this group. Filippovsky's group succeeded in infiltrating through the marshes and conducted several raids against the German rear areas, which stung Konrad into action. Drawing upon the slim resources of both German corps, Konrad was able to gather two infantry battalions from 46.Infanterie-Division, one mountain battalion from 1.Gebirgs-Division, the Radfahrer-Regiment 4 and a small Kampfgruppe from 13.Panzer-Division for a counterattack against Filippovsky's group. On 28 February, the attack began as a series of columns probing into the marshland, which quickly cut off Filippovsky's troops, who were virtually standing in frozen water. Running out of ammunition and food, Filippovsky begged for support. Rear-Admiral Sergey G. Gorshkov's Azov Flotilla had only been operational at the port of Yeisk for a week but he was able to send three small vessels with 300 tons of supplies to Filippovsky. Nevertheless, this only prolonged the agony as the Germans closed the ring around the two isolated Soviet divisions. In desperation, Filippovsky conducted an unauthorized breakout on 4 March and made it back to Soviet lines with some of his troops. Success did not come cheaply for Konrad's corps though, which suffered 800 casualties holding the Poseidon Line for 12 days. Once Ott's LII Armeekorps was withdrawn, Konrad's XXXXIX Gebirgskorps took control over 17.Armee's left flank north of the Kuban River.

By mid-March, it was clear that the Soviet advance had been completely halted by 17.Armee's defensive positions, which were soon dubbed the 'Blue Line'.[23] The combination of spring rains, heavy casualties and supply problems had robbed the two Soviet fronts of much of their offensive vigour. On 16 March, Stavka ordered

A German squad, armed with an MG34 light machine gun, sets out on patrol in the Lagoon sector in a pneumatic raft. Since they could not maintain a continuous front in the marshes, XXXXIX Gebirgskorps was forced to conduct regular patrols with light watercraft. Obviously, such patrols did not have communications and were on their own if they ran into a larger Soviet force. (Süddeutsche Zeitung, 00404153)

23   Hitler apparently used a blue pencil to mark the defensive perimeter in the Kuban on his map, which became a nickname for the position, which was still officially known as the Gotenkopf-Stellung. Both names were used.

both the Black Sea Group and the North Caucasus Front to shift to the defensive and begin preparations for a major assault to break the German front. Over the next week, the Soviets reorganized their forces and repaired damaged infrastructure to improve their logistic support. The Black Sea Group was incorporated into the North Caucasus Front and Petrov became Maslennikov's deputy. The chaotic Soviet order of battle was simplified when the 46th Army was pulled back into the Stavka Reserve (Rezerv Verhovnogo Glavnokomandovanija – RVGK) and some of its units transferred to Grechko's 56th Army. However, the biggest change was the transfer of the 18th Army, now under General-leytenant Konstantin N. Leselidze, to take charge of the forces in the Malaya Zemlya beachhead. By March, part of the 16th Rifle Corps, two rifle divisions, two naval brigades and an artillery regiment were in the Malaya Zemlya, and Leselidze was promised the 5th Guards Tank Brigade, to give him the power to break out of his beachhead.

Maslennikov submitted his offensive plans to destroy 17.Armee to Stavka on 22 March and Stalin quickly approved them. Under Maslennikov's plan, Grechko's 56th Army was going to make the main attack against Gruppe Angelis' positions at Krymskaya, while the 9th, 37th and 58th armies made supporting attacks against 17.Armee's left flank. Maslennikov was given less than two weeks to prepare for the operation, which would begin on 4 April.

The Germans also used the late March respite to reorganize 17.Armee and prepare for future operations. In February and March, 17.Armee suffered a total of 13,882 casualties, including 4,098 dead or missing, but received few replacements. Supplies were low and the material condition of the army's remaining vehicles and heavy weapons was poor. Yet once von Manstein's Heeresgruppe Süd recaptured Kharkov and stabilized the crisis in the Donbass region, there were continual efforts by other commands to cull units from 17.Armee. The OKH succeeded in gradually extracting LII Armeekorps and several divisions out of the Kuban to send to von Manstein, beginning with the 46. and 198.Infanterie-Division. The Romanian 2nd Mountain Division was also withdrawn from the Kuban and stationed in the Crimea. Oddly, 1.Gebirgs-Division was sent to Greece for anti-partisan work. Troops were often flown out via the Luftwaffe airlift but vehicles and heavy equipment went by sea, which took weeks. Typically, it took a month to pull a division out of the Kuban, reorganize it in the Crimea, then send it to the gaining command. Although Hitler would not allow 17.Armee to be withdrawn from the Kuban, he allowed von Manstein to pick some of its most effective formations, leaving Ruoff with a much less capable force.

Ruoff's main concern was the Malaya Zemlya lodgement, which he wanted to crush as soon as possible. He began planning a counter-offensive known as Operation *Neptun* in late March and pulled 4.Gebirgs-Division out of the line to reorganize so it could spearhead this effort. By this point, the Soviets had roughly 20,000 troops in the lodgement and had fortified their position. Ruoff only had a limited amount of heavy artillery and armoured vehicles, which meant that he lacked the resources to overcome a strong enemy defence on his own. Since the situation on the rest of the Eastern Front had stabilized, the Luftwaffe agreed to transfer an air corps to the region in April to support the operation. From this point on, both sides focused their efforts in the Kuban on three non-contiguous sectors: the Temryuk/Lagoon sector along the Sea of Azov, the Krymskaya sector in the centre and the coastal sector around Novorossiysk.

A German command post near a village in the Kuban during a bombardment. Note the spools of communications wire in the foreground. Signal troops were expected to repair breaks in the wire caused by enemy bombardment. (Süddeutsche Zeitung, 00404132)

A Soviet 152mm ML-20 howitzer prepares to fire. The North Caucasus Front amassed a considerable amount of artillery for its offensives against the Blue Line, in an effort to pulverize German defences. However, the Front never formed artillery divisions or corps and the bulk of its weapons consisted of light 76mm guns and 122mm medium howitzers. (Courtesy of the Central Museum of the Armed Forces, Moscow via Stavka)

While building up for larger operations, neither side was particularly satisfied with the situation north of the Kuban River. The Soviet 9th Army kept up the pressure on the left flank of Konrad's XXXXIX Gebirgskorps and Konrad finally abandoned the strongpoint at Slavyansk on 22 March. Konrad's troops withdrew 20km to the Anna Stellung, centred on the town of Anastasiyevskaya, 8km north of the Kuban River. On 26 March, the Soviets mounted a major attack against 50.Infanterie-Division with two rifle divisions and about 40 Lee medium tanks from the 92nd Tank Brigade and 132nd Independent Tank Battalion. The Soviet attack was conducted across open, waterlogged terrain and German artillery and automatic weapons easily smashed the attackers. Three days later, the Soviets attacked again, with similar results. However, the appearance of Ju-87 Stuka dive-bombers from I./Sturzkampfgeschwader 3, based in Kerch, to support the defenders should have alerted the Soviets that the Luftwaffe was returning to the region. On 31 March, the Germans abandoned Anastasiyevskaya and occupied positions just north of the river (the Susana Stellung). Even before Konrad was settled into his new positions, the 9th Army attacked again and was repulsed. In a week of fighting, Konrad estimated that he had inflicted about 10:1 casualties on the 9th Army, including over 3,000 dead and 40 tanks knocked out.

While the Red Army was slowly advancing into the Kuban, the VVS-ChF mounted several attacks against 17.Armee's supply lines across the Kerch Strait. The Il-4 bombers of 5th Guards Mine-Torpedo Aviation Regiment dropped about 65 mines into the Kerch Strait area, primarily AMG-1 contact mines. These mines were responsible for sinking the German MFP *F371* on 9 March, followed by two more MFPs sunk on 14 and 15 March. Considering that the Germans only had about 20 MFPs employed on the Kerch–Anapa route at the time, these were serious losses that threatened the German logistic pipeline to the Kuban and the Kriegsmarine was forced to quickly shift R-boats and minesweeping trawlers to Kerch to deal with this threat. However, the value of air-delivered minelaying was not appreciated by the Soviet high command, which was more focused on the land battle. Neither Stalin nor Zhukov spent much time considering the air–sea battle over the Black Sea. The VVS-ChF only had a limited supply of air-delivered mines, and even when they received some British naval mines via Lend-Lease, they were used to mine Romanian coastal waters, not the Kerch Strait.

Meanwhile, Soviet intelligence failed to detect that the headquarters of Generalleutnant Alfred Mahnke's Fliegerkorps I arrived in Simferopol in the Crimea on the last day of March. With the situation on the main front settled for the moment, Luftflotte 4 was transferring strong forces to the Crimea to support 17.Armee and they arrived at airfields around Kerch and in the Kuban. Altogether, the Luftwaffe was able to assemble over 540 combat aircraft (135 fighters, 211 bombers and 198 Stukas) in the region for a period of six weeks before they would be needed to support the main event: Operation *Zitadelle*, the offensive against the Kursk salient.

THE SOVIET SPRING OFFENSIVES, 4 APRIL–5 MAY 1943

The first battle of Krymskaya, 4–28 April

With marshland and rivers on the German left and mountains and the city of Novorossiysk on the German right, the only place where 17.Armee's front was really assailable was in the centre around the city of Krymskaya. Gruppe Angelis (XXXXIV Armeekorps) was the cork in the bottle that blocked a 12km-wide mobility corridor between the Kuban River and the mountains to the south.

After evacuating the forward position at Abinskaya, Rupp's 97.Jäger-Division established a 10km-wide front east of Krymskaya, forward of the Adagum River. German *Pioniere* created a formidable line of fieldworks and wooden bunkers around Krymskaya and by late March the town was prepared for a 360-degree defence. After several weeks of preparation, most troops in forward positions had underground shelters with 80cm-thick overhead protection that rendered them safe against all but a direct hit from heavy artillery. All automatic weapons and mortars were dug in and carefully sited into interlocking fields of fire. There was also time to lay some S- and T-mines, as well as barbed-wire obstacles. Although the Krymskaya position was hardly impregnable, it did incorporate all the lessons that the Germans had learned about defensive combat and would require a skilful and deliberate assault to crack.

The Soviet VVS received nearly 100 American-built P-39 'Kobra' fighters in early 1943, which were used in air combat over the Krymskaya sector in April and May 1943. Here, a P-39 is being refuelled at a forward airstrip. Unlike most Lend-Lease aircraft, Soviet pilots had a high regard for the P-39 and one-third of all Soviet aces flew the P-39 at some point in their career. (Author's collection)

Kampfgruppe Otte (I., III./Jäger-Regiment 207 and the Romanian 1st Battalion, 94th Infantry Regiment) protected the division's left flank, while Major Friedrich Höhne commanded a Kampfgruppe (II./Jäger-Regiment 204 and Grenadier-Bataillon zbV 560) that held the critical centre section around the train station. Since Rupp's division only had two regiments, his right flank was held by a Romanian battle group (1st Battalion, 95th Infantry Regiment from 19th Infantry Division and I./Jäger-Regiment 204) under Colonel Grigore Mosteoru. Rupp kept a substantial tactical reserve inside Krymskaya, consisting of the III./Jäger-Regiment 204, the II./Jäger-Regiment 207 and a Romanian battalion. Behind Rupp's HKL there were about 60 artillery pieces and two batteries of Nebelwerfers pre-registered on all enemy avenues of approach. This position was the closest 17.Armee came to establishing the Gotenkopf Stellung that Hitler imagined could indefinitely hold the Kuban.

Angelis deployed Generalleutnant Emil Vogel's 101.Jäger-Division to protect the northern approaches to Krymskaya on Rupp's left flank and 9.Infanterie Division to hold the right flank south of the city. Angelis kept a few infantry companies and a handful of assault guns in tactical reserve, but otherwise was dependent upon 17.Armee for more substantial help if his front was breached. Ruoff had 13.Panzer-Division's Kampfgruppe Brux ready to deploy, with its few remaining tanks and Panzergrenadiers.

Grechko's 56th Army assembled two main shock groups to overwhelm Rupp's division: a northern group consisting of three divisions (2nd Guards Rifle Division, 20th and 83rd Mountain Rifle divisions) and a southern group spearheaded by General-major Ivan A. Rubanyuk's 10th Guards Rifle Corps and the 61st and 383rd Rifle divisions. Grechko's offensive would begin with

Soviet troops removing enemy mines from a beach in the Kuban at low tide. The soldier in the foreground has disarmed a Tellermine 42. Note the two scouts in the background with camouflage capes. (Author's collection)

a preparatory bombardment by over 500 artillery pieces, but ammunition was in short supply. Amazingly, Grechko had very little armour or sappers attached to his assault groups and Maslennikov's plan was essentially a 1916-style attack. Indeed, Maslennikov failed to properly weight his main effort and allowed artillery, engineer and tank units to remain idle in other sectors. North of Krymskaya, the 37th Army would mount a supporting attack against 101.Jäger-Division with 9th Mountain Rifle Division and some Valentine tanks from the 151st Tank Brigade. The 4th VA and 5th VA would support the offensive with about 450 aircraft.

At 0715hrs on 4 April, Grechko's offensive began with a 60-minute artillery barrage that fell primarily on Rupp's outpost line. Soviet forward observers could not identify the main German positions in the HKL and the artillery simply conducted an area bombardment. Then Rubanyuk's 10th Guards Rifle Corps surged forward across hundreds of yards of open ground along the rail line to strike the forward positions of Kampfgruppe Höhne. Artillery from the German Artillerie-Regiment 81 and the Romanian Artillery Regiment 37 fired barrages right in front on the Axis positions, but the Soviet infantry came on in waves. The II./Jäger-Regiment 204 was surprised when Soviet infantry suddenly appeared in their positions and overran one of its forward companies; the commander of 6.Kompanie was captured. The I./Jäger-Regiment 204 was also hard hit and lost most of its 1.Kompanie. After hours of heavy fighting, Rubanyuk's 10th Guards Rifle Corps managed to push forward about 1,500 metres along the rail line and threatened to split Höhne's two battalions. On Höhne's right flank, Colonel Mosteoru's Romanian infantry were also hard-pressed. However, Kampfgruppe Otte repulsed the attack by 2nd Guards Rifle Division, which enabled Rupp to focus his attention on his centre and right. With the help of an assault gun battery and all the division artillery, a battalion-size counterattack by Hauptmann Georg Gebhardt's III./Jäger-Regiment 204 managed to prevent 10th Guards Rifle Corps from breaking through and gradually pushed them back. Late afternoon showers reduced visibility for the Soviet artillery and hindered movement, which allowed the defenders to restore their original front line. Meanwhile, Vogel's 101.Jäger-Division had fended off the supporting attack by the 37th Army and the entire Soviet offensive ground to a halt. Rupp estimated that his division had killed about 1,500 Soviet troops and knocked out ten tanks, with another 253 Soviets taken prisoner. Artillerie-Regiment 81 fired 5,600 rounds during the day – about 11 times the normal daily allotment.

Surprised by this rebuff, Maslennikov was unable to resume his offensive the next day, which enabled Ruoff to commit Kampfgruppe Brux from 13.Panzer-Division to reinforce Gruppe Angelis' defence. On 6 April, Grechko resumed the offensive but his attacks quickly fizzled out. The rapid failure of Maslennikov's offensive caught Stavka by surprise. Maslennikov was given a week to reorganize, then he resumed his offensive late on 14 April. Rather than a single main effort, this time Maslennikov directed the 58th, 9th, 37th and 56th armies to attack across the width of 17.Armee's front line, hoping to find a weak spot somewhere. Instead, he simply dissipated his combat power and failed to achieve anything. On 15 April, Grechko threw his veteran 10th Guards Rifle Corps into the attack once again and managed to reach the outskirts of Krymskaya. Pressing hard against Kampfgruppe Höhne, Rubanyuk's 10th Guards Rifle Corps reached

The Soviet 9th Army tried repeatedly to infiltrate through the marshy Lagoon area and outflank the Germans, but every attempt was repulsed with heavy casualties. Here, Soviet infantrymen try to use personal flotation rings to move through one of the marshes. Once spotted, German machine guns and mortars would rip these infiltration groups apart. (From the fonds of the RGAKFD in Krasnogorsk via Stavka)

the train station on the eastern outskirts of Krymskaya on the morning of 16 April, threatening to split Rupp's front. Yet now the Luftwaffe appeared in force, flying more than 1,500 sorties over the Kuban while Kampfgruppe Brux spearheaded an armoured counterattack to restore the front. German Stukas pounded the Soviet assault formations and the Germans claimed to have knocked out 48 Soviet tanks. By late on 16 April, it was clear that the second round of Maslennikov's offensive had collapsed without achieving any of its objectives.

Stunned by the complete failure of the North Caucasus Front's offensive, Stavka sent Marshal Zhukov and a high-level delegation to the Kuban to coordinate remedial measures.

Zhukov's delegation included an unusual amount of brass: Marshal Aleksandr A. Novikov, commander of the VVS, Admiral Nikolai G. Kuznetsov, head of the Soviet Navy, and General-leytenant Sergei M. Shtemenko, head of operations in the General Staff. Zhukov was scathing in his report to Stalin and described Maslennikov's forces as 'carelessly and casually organized', which was not far from the truth. Novikov reorganized the 4th VA and convinced Stavka to release additional air reserves for service in the Kuban, including the 3rd Fighter Aviation Corps, 2nd Bomber Aviation Corps, the 2nd Composite Aviation Corps and the 287th Fighter Aviation Division; this amounted to about 460 fighters, 165 bombers and 170 Il-2 Sturmoviks. On 24 April, the 5th VA headquarters was transferred to the Steppe Front and all its units attached to the 4th VA. With the aircraft from 5th VA and the Stavka reserves, the VVS would have almost 1,200 aircraft to support the next Kuban offensive.

On the ground, the scheme of manoeuvre remained essentially the same, with Grechko's 56th Army as the main effort, but Zhukov also demanded that the 9th and 37th armies make significant supporting attacks to prevent 17.Armee from just focusing on one sector. In particular, Zhukov ordered the 9th Army to assemble small boats so it could attack through the marshy Lagoon area and cross the Kuban River. In order to reinforce the main effort, Zhukov requested substantial reinforcements from the Stavka reserves to augment 56th Army's firepower. Due to Zhukov's intervention, Grechko was provided with two regiments of self-propelled artillery with 40 assault guns, four Guards Mortar battalions with 72 300mm multiple rocket launchers and 50 Lend-Lease tanks, as well as 3,000 veteran troops. Zhukov's plan for the next offensive against the Krymskaya position was quickly approved on 24 April and he was given five additional days before beginning the operation in order for reinforcements and additional supplies to arrive.

Operation *Neptun*, 17–25 April 1943

Ruoff watched while Maslennikov's first series of offensive jabs against Krymskaya failed, and then decided the time was ripe to activate his own plan to crush the Malaya Zemlya bridgehead with a counter-offensive designated Operation *Neptun*. By this point, General-leytenant Konstantin N. Leselidze's 18th Army in the bridgehead had grown to more than 20,000 troops with its own artillery and tank support. Wetzel's V Armeekorps was tasked with conducting the ground counter-offensive and he was provided with 4.Gebirgs-Division, 125.Infanterie-Division and parts of three Romanian divisions (6th Cavalry, 10th and 19th Infantry), supported by Sturmgeschütz-Abteilung 249 and three battalions of Heeresartillerie (with 9 x 21cm, 12 x 10cm and 16 x 15cm howitzers). Altogether, Wetzel had 28,000 troops, of whom half were Romanian. Wetzel's forces were barely adequate for the task, but Ruoff expected that the intervention of Mahnke's Fliegerkorps I would tip the balance in favour of the Germans. In addition, the Kriegsmarine was tasked with interdicting Soviet naval supply lines to the beachhead to prevent reinforcements or ammunition from getting through. The five boats of 1.Schnellbootsflotille and seven Italian MAS boats were moved to Anapa to be closer to the enemy supply lines. The Luftwaffe also reinforced its 8.8cm Flak batteries on the north side of Tsemes Bay, in an effort to interfere with Soviet traffic across the bay to the Malaya Zemlya bridgehead.

Wetzel's plan for *Neptun* was unorthodox. The main effort would be undertaken by Generalleutnant Hermann Kress's 4.Gebirgs-Division, which would attack first to seize Mount Myskhako. Once this was accomplished, Generalleutnant Helmut Friebe's 125.Infanterie-Division would attack the centre of the Soviet perimeter, north-east of Fedotovka, and push east to the main north–south road. If this succeeded, part of von Bünau's 73.Infanterie-Division would attack south and recapture Stanichka. Although there were plenty of Romanian troops involved in *Neptun*, most were assigned only supporting roles, such as flank guards. Wetzel was forced to delay the operation several times due to adverse weather, which affected flight operations, but he could not delay for long due to the

German infantry advance behind an assault gun during Operation *Neptun*, the counterattack against the Malaya Zemlya bridgehead in April 1943. The terrain around Mount Myskhako proved challenging, due to dense underbrush such as this and the limited avenues of approach. (Author's collection)

Operation *Neptun*, 17–25 April

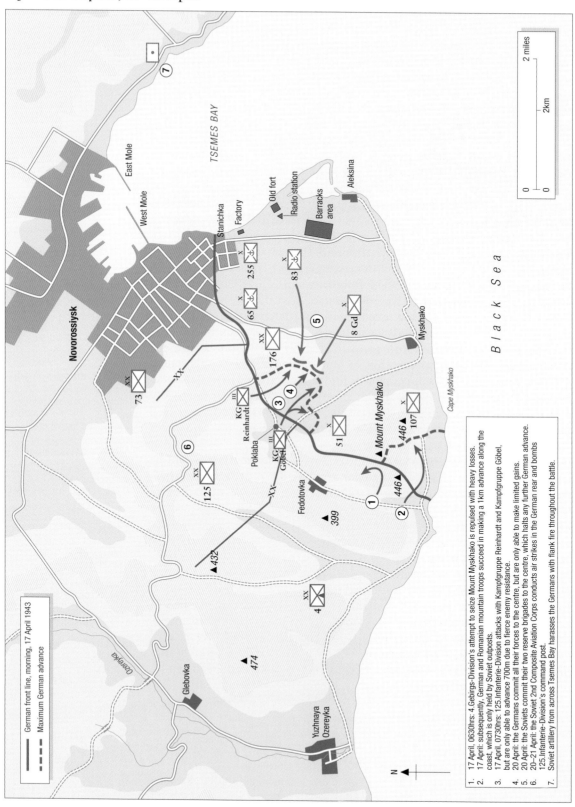

Legend:
— German front line, morning, 17 April 1943
---- Maximum German advance

1. 17 April, 0630hrs: 4.Gebirgs-Division's attempt to seize Mount Myskhako is repulsed with heavy losses.
2. 17 April: subsequently, German and Romanian mountain troops succeed in making a 1km advance along the coast, which is only held by Soviet outposts.
3. 17 April, 0730hrs: 125.Infanterie-Division attacks with Kampfgruppe Reinhardt and Kampfgruppe Göbel, but are only able to advance 700m due to fierce enemy resistance.
4. 20 April: the Germans commit all their forces to the centre, but are only able to make limited gains.
5. 20 April: the Soviets commit their two reserve brigades to the centre, which halts any further German advance.
6. 20–21 April: the Soviet 2nd Composite Aviation Corps conducts air strikes in the German rear and bombs 125.Infanterie-Division's command post.
7. Soviet artillery from across Tsemes Bay harasses the Germans with flank fire throughout the battle.

A German defensive position in the Kuban. Note the flare gun for alert purposes. Here, the Germans clearly can see any enemy approaching for up to a kilometre across open ground, which made it difficult for Soviet troops to reach the German trench lines. (Nik Cornish at www.Stavka.org.uk)

inevitability of another Soviet offensive against Krymskaya. He set 17 April as the date for *Neptun* to begin.

When the sun began rising at 0243hrs on 17 April, it was clear that the weather was not going to cooperate with Wetzel's plan since there was considerable ground fog and 60 per cent cloud cover. Wetzel pushed the start time from 0530hrs back to 0630hrs, but it made no difference. Kress's 4.Gebirgs-Division had assembled five mountain battalions and a Pionier battalion just west of Mount Myskhako. They had to cross a narrow valley which the Soviets had dubbed 'Death Valley' and ascend a very steep and heavily wooded slope. On top of the mountain, Major Dmitri P. Chumina's 2nd Battalion of the 107th Rifle Brigade (Polkovnik T. I. Shumin) was dug in and waiting for them. Mahnke's Fliegerkorps I committed over 150 Ju-87 Stukas and He-111s to the opening attacks and there was virtually no opposition from the VVS, but the Luftwaffe pilots could not see the targets through the clouds. Instead, the bomber formations tried to bomb through the clouds, but without any accuracy. Despite the failure of the heavily anticipated Luftwaffe air support, Kress attacked anyway, supported by his two battalions of 7.5cm mountain guns. Chumina's troops opened fire with machine guns and mortars as the Gebirgsjäger charged up the slopes, inflicting crippling losses. In short order, almost all the German company commanders were casualties and the attack faltered. Several Ju-87 Stukas attempted to bomb the mountain top through the clouds but at least one bomb fell among the Gebirgsjäger instead. Seeing his division being demolished, Kress called off the attack without authorization from Wetzel. The attack had been a fiasco, costing 4.Gebirgs-Division 898 casualties; Gebirgsjäger-Regiment 91 was particularly hard hit.

Before Wetzel was fully aware that Kress's attack had failed, he ordered Friebe's 125.Infanterie-Division to begin its part of the offensive at 0730hrs. The 125.Infanterie-Division had the dubious distinction of being known as the 'Weasel Division' due to its division symbol, but it had gained a good reputation for its performance in the Caucasus campaign. However, the division was now being ordered to attack the Soviet beachhead on its own and without much combat support. The Luftwaffe still could not observe

Heavily armed Soviet naval infantrymen, supported by a heavy machine gun, holding a section of the front in the Malaya Zemlya lodgement. Although the naval infantry had a very good combat reputation, particularly in the defence, most had very little ground combat training. Instead, naval infantry battalions were much larger and better armed than standard Red Army rifle battalions, which gave them better staying power. (Author's collection)

the Soviet positions and could only conduct area bombardment, not close air support. Friebe was supposed to have received Sturmgeschütz-Abteilung 249 to support his attack, but Gruppe Angelis had been reluctant to part with this unit in case of another Soviet attack in their sector, so the promised assault guns did not arrive in time. Friebe attacked with five battalions: Kampfgruppe Reinhardt (Oberst Alfred-Hermann Reinhardt) with two battalions of Grenadier-Regiment 421, and Kampfgruppe Göbel (Oberstleutnant Karl Göbel) with three battalions of Grenadier-Regiment 420. The attack occurred near the boundary of the Soviet 51st Rifle Brigade and the 176th Rifle Division over terrain that was hilly and heavily wooded. Both German *Kampfgruppen* quickly found that Soviet resistance was extremely fierce and their infantry could only make slight progress. Although the attack by 125.Infanterie-Division continued for the rest of the day, neither *Kampfgruppe* was able to advance more than 700m.

Meanwhile, once the sun set at 1615hrs, the Axis tried to implement a complete blockade of the Soviet naval supply lines to the Malaya Zemlya bridgehead. Kapitänleutnant Klassmann's 3.Räumbootsflotille took position off Cape Myskhako with three of his R-boats while Korvettenkapitän Christiansen's 1.Schnellbootsflotille assumed ambush positions south-east of Tsemes Bay. Commander Francesco Mimbelli's 4th MAS Flotilla was sent with six Italian MAS boats to attack enemy coastal shipping near the port of Gelendzhik. The Germans also had 30.Unterseebootsflotille operating from the Romanian port of Constanza, which deployed three Type IIB submarines in the eastern Black Sea during *Neptun*.[24] Although there were frequent encounters with Soviet patrol boats during *Neptun*, the Axis failed to completely stop coastal shipping to the beachhead. As a back-up, Kuznetsov ordered the Black Sea Fleet to employ three of its submarines to deliver supplies to the 18th Army.

After reorganizing his forces, Wetzel decided to continue *Neptun*, focusing on trying to cleave the enemy beachhead in two. Several of Kress's Gebirgsjäger battalions were shifted to join 125.Infanterie-Division's attack, while 4.Gebirgs-Division shifted to the defence. The Romanian 9th Cavalry Regiment (dismounted) was also added. On 20 April, the Germans renewed their offensive with a major push straight down the middle in the 125. Infanterie-Division sector, attempting to drive a wedge between the 51st Rifle Brigade and the 176th Rifle Division. Now Wetzel had two assault gun batteries, two battalions of Nebelwerfer rocket launchers and plenty of close air support, which enabled his assault groups to advance almost 1,000m into

24 By June 1943, the Kriegsmarine had six Type IIB U-boats operational in the Black Sea.

The air battle in the Kuban, April–September 1943

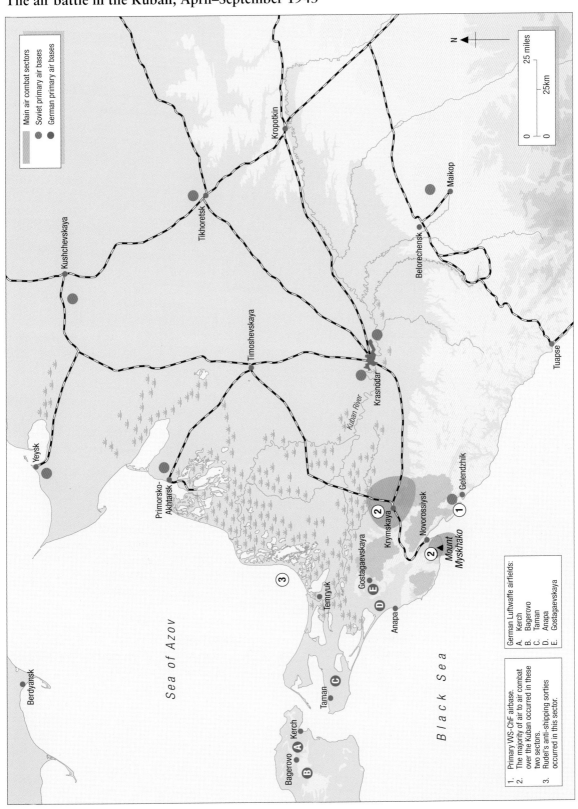

Legend:
Main air combat sectors
Soviet primary air bases
German primary air bases

N

25 miles
0
25km
0

Kropotkin

Maikop

Kushchevskaya

Tikhoretsk

Belorechensk

Timoshevskaya

Krasnodar

Kuban River

Tuapse

Yeysk

Gelendzhik

Primorsko-Akhtarsk

2

Krymskaya

Novorossiysk

1

Berdyansk

Sea of Azov

3

Temryuk

Gostagaevskaya

E

2

Mount Myskhako

D

Anapa

C

Black Sea

Taman

Bagerovo

Kerch

A

B

German Luftwaffe airfields:
A. Kerch
B. Bagerovo
C. Taman
D. Anapa
E. Gostagaevskaya

1. Primary VVS-ChF airbase.
2. The majority of air to air combat over the Kuban occurred in these two sectors.
3. Rudel's anti-shipping sorties occurred in this sector.

53

SOVIET P-39 KOBRAS OVER KRYMSKAYA, 20 APRIL 1943 (PP. 54–55)

In January 1943, the Soviet 4th VA began retraining three of its fighter regiments in the American-made P-39 Airacobra fighter, brought into the Caucasus via Persia. Although already regarded as not a first-line fighter by Anglo-Americans, the VVS pilots quickly took a liking to the P-39's firepower and simple construction, dubbing it the Kobra. In mid-February, the 45th and 298th Fighter Aviation regiments were deployed to the Kuban, each with 32 P-39s, and were later joined by the 16th Guards Fighter Aviation Regiment. All three regiments had a good number of veteran pilots, but at least half had no prior combat experience. At this point, the VVS was operating a mix of P-39D, K and L models.

A number of Soviet aces made their reputations in the P-39, including Kapitan Aleksandr I. Pokryshkin and Kapitan Grigoriy A. Rechkalov of 16th Guards Fighter Aviation Regiment. In April 1943, large-scale air battles erupted over the Krymskaya sector between fighters of the 4th VA and the Luftwaffe's veteran

Jagdflieger of Jagdgeschwader 3 and Jagdgeschwader 53, both equipped with the Bf-109G. Pokryshkin claimed 25 victories over the Kuban in a four-month period, although some of these claims are difficult to verify. About 50 P-39s were lost to enemy action, but surprisingly, the P-39s held their own against the slightly faster Bf-109Gs and certainly downed a number of them.

In this scene, Pokryshkin's P-39D-2 (1) is engaging a Bf-109G-2 fighter (2) from Jagdgeschwader 52 over the front line near Krymskaya (3), with the Black Sea (4) in the background. The Kobra's 20mm cannon has a low rate of fire, but combined with the two .50-cal machine guns in the wings, provides devastating firepower that rips into the German fighter.

Many Soviet pilots liked the P-39 Kobra and it was the most popular of the Lend-Lease aircraft flown by the VVS, and it remained in service until 1949. In contrast, two regiments flew the Spitfire Mark Vb over the Kuban from May to July 1943, but it was soon phased out of Soviet service.

the enemy front line. However, the Soviet units on both flanks held firm and Leselidze committed his two reserve units – the 8th Guards Rifle Brigade and the 83rd Naval Infantry Brigade – to stop the German advance. Marshal Novikov also ordered Naumenko's 4th VA and Goriunov's 5th VA to commit their aircraft en masse to disrupt Luftwaffe close air support. Novikov had succeeded in getting Stavka to send strong aviation reinforcements to the Kuban and General-major Evgeniy I. Savitskiy's 3rd Fighter Aviation Corps had just arrived in theatre with six regiments of Yak fighters. Now the VVS had a 5:1 numerical superiority in fighters, some of which were flown by veteran pilots. In mid-morning, Savitsky's fighters appeared over the Malaya Zemlya bridgehead and engaged Fliegerkorps I head-on. One *Staffel* of He-111 bombers was attacked and three aircraft were damaged, which compelled the others to abort their mission.

These actions over the beachhead represented the beginning of several weeks of intense air battles over the Kuban, which drew in some of the best pilots on both sides. The veteran aces of Jagdgeschwader 3 and Jagdgeschwader 52 shot down dozens of Soviet aircraft, but German Stuka units also began to suffer significant losses and became more cautious. General-major Ivan T. Eremenko's 2nd Composite Aviation Corps also made a strong appearance over the battlefield by conducting two large raids with IL-2 Sturmoviks against German artillery positions. While the Soviets claimed that the intervention of the VVS tipped the balance against *Neptun*, Fliegerkorps I still held the tactical edge and inflicted much higher losses upon the enemy. Fliegerkorps I did lose at least 21 Bf-109G fighters, 26 Ju-87D Stukas and 21 bombers to enemy action during April 1943, but the 4th VA losses were several times that number. Nevertheless, Wetzel was discouraged by the fierce enemy resistance and decided to halt his offensive.

Without clear air superiority and only modest ground forces, Wetzel's Operation *Neptun* degenerated into a static slugging match that accomplished nothing. The Germans continued to attack for another week, but made no further gains. The Soviet defences were far too strong to overcome with a couple of depleted infantry divisions and all Wetzel had succeeded in accomplishing was the creation of a small salient jutting into enemy lines. By the end of the month, Wetzel pulled 4.Gebirgs-Division and most of the depleted assault formations out of the line and assigned Romanian units to hold more of the perimeter around the Soviet lodgement. Thereafter, Wetzel was content to pound away at the lodgement with his artillery and occasional bomber raids. Operation *Neptun* had failed miserably and this failure made 17.Armee's coastal flank a constant source of concern.

On the Soviet side, the defeat of Operation *Neptun* was proclaimed a major victory by the 18th Army's new senior commissar, Polkovnik Leonid

A 76.2mm ZIS-3 gun in the Malaya Zemlya today. The Soviets were able to land a number of ZIS-3 guns in the beachhead, which were well suited to the defensive mission since they could be moved around easily and concealed. Furthermore, the ZIS-3 could fire either armour-piercing or high-explosive rounds, which gave it a dual anti-tank and anti-personnel capability. (Author's collection)

The first and second battles of Krymskaya, 4 April–4 May 1943

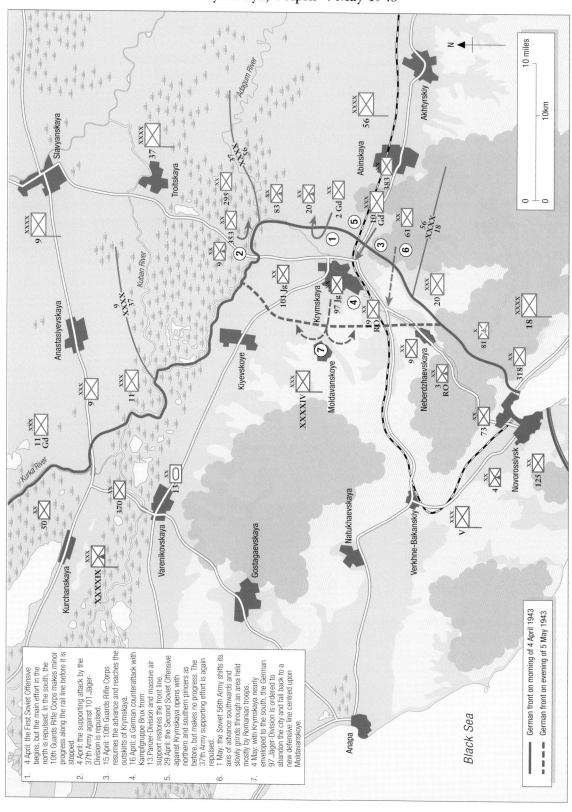

1. 4 April: the First Soviet Offensive begins; but the main effort in the north is repulsed. In the south, the 10th Guards Rifle Corps makes minor progress along the rail line before it is stopped.
2. 4 April: the supporting attack by the 37th Army against 101.Jäger-Division is repulsed.
3. 15 April: 10th Guards Rifle Corps resumes the advance and reaches the outskirts of Krymskaya.
4. 16 April: a German counterattack with Kampfgruppe Brux from 13.Panzer-Division and massive air support restores the front line.
5. 29 April: the Second Soviet Offensive against Krymskaya opens with northern and southern pincers as before, but makes no progress. The 37th Army supporting effort is again repulsed.
6. 1 May: the Soviet 56th Army shifts its axis of advance southwards and slowly grinds through an area held mostly by Romanian troops.
7. 4 May: with Krymskaya nearly enveloped to the south, the German 97.Jäger-Division is ordered to abandon the city and fall back to a new defensive line centred upon Moldavanskoye.

— German front on morning of 4 April 1943
--- German front on evening of 5 May 1943

58

Brezhnev, who 21 years later would rise to become General Secretary of the Communist Party. Brezhnev made a great deal of his alleged heroism in the Malaya Zemlya in his post-war memoirs, although much of this was likely fabricated to enhance his military credentials. Whatever his exact contributions to defending the beachhead – which were mostly speech-making – Brezhnev's participation in the fight for the Malaya Zemlya beachhead ensured that this aspect of the Kuban campaign would be remembered and enshrouded in heroic legend.

The second battle of Krymskaya, 29 April–5 May

As part of Zhukov's plan for the next offensive, the North Caucasus Front formed the Titov Tank Group with the 5th Guards Tank Brigade and the 63rd Tank Brigade. The North Caucasus Front had generally dispersed its armour in the infantry support role, but Zhukov wanted to mass at least 60 tanks to support the main effort. He also made an attempt to mass the Front's artillery by deploying 15 artillery regiments along a 10km-wide breakthrough zone in the centre of the 56th Army sectors. However, apparently Zhukov had doubts about the reliability of Grechko's troops and took unusual steps to reinforce discipline. Zhukov had already made criticisms to Stavka that non-Russian troops in the North Caucasus Front were not fully reliable. Prior to the offensive, the Germans reported that Armenian, Georgian and Ukrainian troops were regularly deserting to them, often with important information about Soviet preparations. As a result, the 1st NKVD Special Purpose Division was positioned behind the 56th Army. Ostensibly, this very large NKVD division – which included six regiments – was assigned to act as an exploitation force once a breakthrough was achieved. In reality, the NKVD troops were there to discourage lapses in discipline by the troops of the 56th Army.

Gruppe Angelis made no major changes to its dispositions in front of Krymskaya. Kampfgruppe Otte still anchored the northern flank atop Hill 30.1 and Colonel Mosteoru's Romanian battlegroup held the southern flank. The railway embankment provided a valuable boost to the defence, with fighting positions dug in just behind it. Kampfgruppe Brux provided the only mobile reserve.

At 0740hrs on 29 April, 56th Army began its second offensive with a 100-minute-long preparation by artillery and air attacks. Most of the available aircraft were assigned to the 4th VA, which conducted 1,268 sorties in a single day. However, the German artillery was not suppressed and Fliegerkorps I was able to intervene in force over the battlefield, although the Luftwaffe only flew 539 sorties on 29 April. Intense squadron-size dogfights occurred in a narrow 25km-wide sector around Krymskaya.

Hauptmann Hans-Ulrich Rudel tested the first cannon-equipped Ju-87 Stuka in the Kuban in May and used it against Soviet small boat traffic. Rudel's Kanonvogel evolved into the Ju-87G just in time for the battle of Kursk in July 1943. (Bundesarchiv, Bild 101I-655-5976-04, Foto: Helmut Grosse)

Grechko's 56th Army attacked with two shock groups. The northern group consisted of General-major Mikhail F. Tikhonov's 11th Guards Rifle Corps (2nd and 32nd Guards Rifle divisions) and the 383rd Guards Rifle Division, while the southern group consisted of General-major Rubanyuk's 10th Guards Rifle Corps and the 216th and 317th Rifle divisions. Titov's Tank Group was deployed to support Tikhonov's wing and Grechko kept the 61st Rifle Division and 328th Rifle Division in reserve to support any breakthrough.

Tikhonov's troops had to cross several hundred metres of flat, open terrain to reach the German positions and they were mercilessly pounded by mortars and automatic-weapon fire from Kampfgruppe Otte. The 2nd Guards Rifle Division was repulsed outright but the 32nd Guards Rifle Division managed to reach the German wire and a combat outpost in the Pytiletka State Farm on the east side of the railroad embankment was abandoned. Nevertheless, the Soviet northern pincer had failed. Rubanyuk's southern shock group, led by the 317th Rifle Division, was able to gain about 1,000m near the boundary between 97.Jäger-Division and 9.Infanterie-Division. In response, Angelis committed Kampfgruppe Brux, which managed to temporarily restore the original HKL. Heavy fighting continued on 30 April, although without much change. Tikhonov mounted a night attack against Kampfgruppe Otte, which also failed. Rubanyuk's 10th Guards Rifle Corps continued to make minor gains on Rupp's right flank.

Meanwhile, General-major Petr M. Kozlov's 37th Army made minor attacks against 101.Jäger-Division north of Krymskaya, but failed to achieve any success. Two of the soldiers involved in repelling these attacks were Feldwebel Johann Schwerdfeger, a platoon leader in I./Jäger-Regiment 228, and Oberschütze Willi Heinrich. Schwerdfeger was a highly experienced combat veteran and was awarded the Ritterkreuz des Eisernen Kreuzes for his leadership during this phase of the Kuban campaign. After the war, Heinrich wrote the novel *The Willing Flesh* (1955) and Schwerdfeger was likely the basis for the character Sergeant Steiner in the film *The Cross of*

Soviet artillery pounds a village in the Kuban just prior to an assault. Although the North Caucasus Front had plenty of artillery by mid-1943, its artillery preparations often failed to suppress German defences due to poor planning. Typically, Soviet observers could not see the actual German HKL and simply directed fire into the enemy's security zone. (Süddeutsche Zeitung, 00404160)

Iron (1977).[25] Although the Kuban campaign is largely forgotten today, this one aspect of it has managed to remain in the public consciousness.

Zhukov decided to reinforce success, rather than failure and ordered the attack to shift south along the 10th Guards Rifle Corps axis of advance. Slowly, Rubanyuk's forces ground forward towards the southern outskirts of Krymskaya. At 0530hrs on 1 May, Soviet artillery pounded the Romanian battlegroup south of Krymskaya, then Rubanyuk's 10th Guards Rifle Corps attacked. Yet despite the fierce pounding, the Axis line held. Zhukov continued to urge the 56th Army onward, with more attacks on 2 and 3 May, which inched forwards to the west towards the town of Neberdzhaevskaya. On 3 May, the Pe-2s of Ushakov's 2nd Bomber Aviation Corps bombed Rupp's artillery relentlessly, while the Il-2 Sturmoviks of Yeremenko's 2nd Composite Aviation Corps tried to blast a way through the German positions.

By 4 May, Rupp's 97.Jäger-Division was still holding firm, but it was now in a salient with the 37th Army to the north and the bulk of the 56th Army to the south. Some Soviet troops had already cut the rail line to Novorossiysk and it was clear that Krymskaya was being outflanked, so Angelis requested permission to withdraw several kilometres westwards. During the night of 4/5 May, Rupp's 97.Jäger-Division quietly evacuated Krymskaya and withdrew to a new line known as the D-Stellung.

Oddly, Zhukov ordered the offensive to continue even after Krymskaya was liberated. Grechko's 56th Army was clearly exhausted and it staggered after the retreating Germans without any vigour. When the 56th Army reached the D-Stellung, which was already occupied, the offensive sputtered out and Zhukov finally called a halt on 10 May. Having accomplished something noteworthy with the liberation of Krymskaya, Zhukov now returned to Moscow on 12 May in order to prepare for the impending German offensive against the Kursk salient. Right after Zhukov left, Maslennikov was relieved of command and Petrov was put in charge of the North Caucasus Front. In addition, the commanders of the 9th and 37th armies – Koroteev and Kozlov – were ordered to switch commands, apparently to try and generate more activity in these sectors. The second major Soviet offensive in the Kuban had succeeded in bending, but not breaking the German line and it had required a massive effort by the North Caucasus Front to get three Axis divisions to retreat a distance of 10km.

Holding the northern flank, 29 March–31 May

While the 56th Army had been smashing itself against the German defences around Krymskaya for six weeks, the Soviet 9th and 37th armies gained no ground against the enemy's northern flank along the Kuban River. The 37th Army, under Kozlov, had been reduced to just three rifle divisions and stripped of most of its artillery. Consequently, Kozlov's supporting attacks against the German 370.Infanterie-Division's position on the Kuban River were too puny to accomplish its assigned mission of crossing the river. However, the relentless attacks had been costly for the Germans in terms of resources and casualties. In the first few days of April, 50.Infanterie-Division fired off 11,000 artillery rounds and requested dozens of Stuka sorties to fend off the Soviet attacks, but still suffered 237 casualties. After a brief respite, the 9th Army renewed its offensive on 17 April, and in four days Konrad's

---

25 Schwerdfeger (1914–2015) served as a front-line infantryman in the Wehrmacht from 1934 to 1945 and was awarded the Oak Leaves to his Iron Cross in 1944. He survived the war and made it to the age of 101.

A German 8cm mortar crew in the Kuban, June 1943. German mortar crews were able to quickly put down a very lethal barrage on enemy troops advancing in the open. Note that the mortar position is not dug in very deeply itself. (Bildarchiv Preussischer Kulturbesitz, 50071984)

XXXXIX Gebirgskorps suffered over 1,100 casualties. The hardest hit was 370.Infanterie-Division, which by 25 April was reduced to seven very weak infantry battalions, varying between 20 and 38 per cent of authorized strength.

Nevertheless, Zhukov was unaware of German casualties. All he could see was that neither the 9th nor 37th armies gained any ground in weeks of fighting. He assessed Kozlov as displaying 'weak leadership', but the truth was that the 37th Army had been reduced to little more than a rifle corps and the waterlogged terrain in its sector was abysmal. Zhukov was expecting too much from too little.

Stavka had greater hope for Koroteev's 9th Army, which had the 9th and 11th Rifle corps and two rifle divisions opposing Generalleutnant Friedrich Schmidt's 50.Infanterie-Division north of the Kuban River. Schmidt's division occupied the Katinka Stellung, which was a series of *Stützpunkte* (strongpoints) behind the Jäger Canal east of Kurchanskaya. Schmidt had just six infantry battalions from Infanterie-Regiment 121 and Infanterie-Regiment 123 holding his HKL east of Lake Kurchansky, supported by the remaining 23 howitzers in Artillerie-Regiment 150. However, Schmidt's left flank did not extend to the coast and this area was screened by Kampfgruppe Münchow, with about 400 troops from Wach-Bataillon 602 and 617 and 500 troops from Radfahr-Bataillon 4. Despite repeated attempts, Koroteev's infantry could not break Schmidt's HKL because of the open nature of the terrain; German mortars and automatic weapons slaughtered Soviet infantry attempting to cross the Jäger Canal.

Stymied on the direct approach, Koroteev repeatedly tried to outflank the enemy by infiltrating troops through the Lagoon area along the Sea of Azov. Initially, this sector had belonged to the 58th Army, but after that formation was shifted to coastal defence duties, the 9th Army was made responsible for the Azov Sea coastline, as well. Once spring arrived, the marshes became a sea of thick reeds, with small islands scattered here and there. Kampfgruppe Münchow had patrols and strongpoints on the coast, but there was no front line in the marshes themselves. On 1 May, Gorshkov's Azov Flotilla was able to land 238 troopers from the 34th NKVD Motorized Regiment on the Verbyanaya Spit 12km north-east of the port of Temryuk and this raid was claimed as a tactical success. Encouraged by this brief foray, the 9th Army began sending brigade-size forces by small boats into the coastal marshes in order to surprise and capture some of the German outposts, which were usually platoon size. Soviet infiltrators had some success and managed to capture one strongpoint. Soon, Soviet patrols were threatening the approaches to the port of Temryuk. In response, Konrad's XXXXIX Gebirgskorps formed Kampfgruppe Brücker (I. and III./Grenadier-Regiment 419 from 125.Infanterie-Division) on 5 May to reinforce the coastal area. Ruoff was concerned that the Soviets might attempt an amphibious landing on the Azov coast in order to cut the Axis line of communications to the

Taman Peninsula. In consequence, 17.Armee concentrated 4,500 German and Romanian troops in the Taman Peninsula to guard against this contingency and called this Operation *Seehund* (*Seal*).

Konrad also called upon the Luftwaffe to assist him in preventing the Soviets from turning his left flank. Fw-189 reconnaissance planes were used to spot enemy coastal activity, then air strikes mounted by Ju-87s, Ju-88s and Fw-190s. The small boats were difficult to hit with bombs, but Hauptmann Hans-Ulrich Rudel arrived with a modified Ju-87, equipped with two 3.7cm cannon. Beginning around 1 May, Rudel began conducting low-level attacks against Soviet coastal traffic and was able to score direct hits on enemy boats. He claimed the destruction of 70 enemy boats in about a week, although this cannot be confirmed. It is clear, though, that the 9th Army suffered heavy losses to enemy air attack. By mid-May, Koroteev's infiltration into the marshes had stalled far short of Temryuk and it was proving difficult to supply units as boats were lost and traffic interrupted. The 9th Rifle Corps was dispersed throughout the marshes and had negligible fire support.

On 22 May, Konrad issued an order for Operation *Venedig* (*Venice*) to counterattack the Soviet 43rd Rifle Brigade with two assault groups formed by two battalions from Schmidt's 50.Infanterie-Division. In a series of small counterattacks, Konrad's forces began slowly mopping up the enemy forces in the marshes, inflicting heavy losses. German airpower was the trump card, smashing Soviet resistance on the ground without much interference from the 4th VA, which was focused on the Krymskaya sector.

A German infantry patrol advances cautiously into a marshy area in the Lagoon along the Sea of Azov. Superior small unit leadership gave the Germans a distinct edge in this kind of tactical combat, whereas Soviet small unit leaders had not been trained with independent operations in mind. (Author's collection)

German troops advancing into a Kuban village while artillery pounds the enemy only a few hundred metres away. When terrain was lost to the enemy, the Germans were quick to mount counterattacks to recover it – often with just a few platoons of whichever troops were available. (Süddeutsche Zeitung, 00404133)

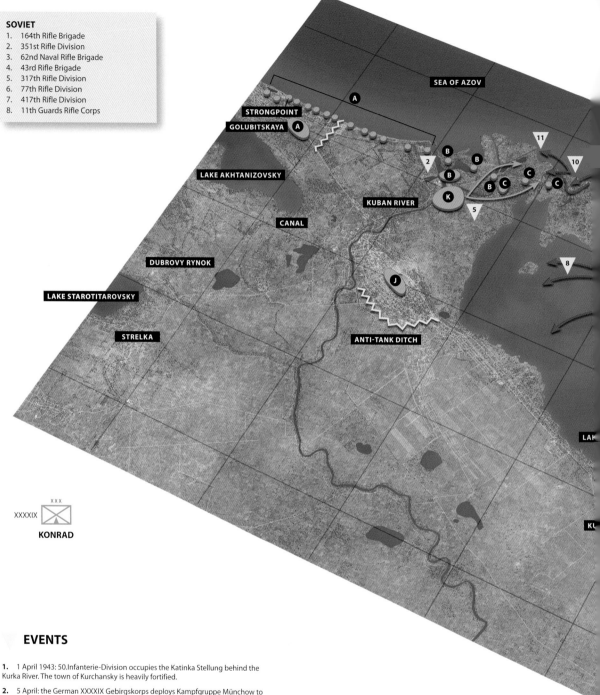

SOVIET

1. 164th Rifle Brigade
2. 351st Rifle Division
3. 62nd Naval Rifle Brigade
4. 43rd Rifle Brigade
5. 317th Rifle Division
6. 77th Rifle Division
7. 417th Rifle Division
8. 11th Guards Rifle Corps

SEA OF AZOV

STRONGPOINT

GOLUBITSKAYA

LAKE AKHTANIZOVSKY

KUBAN RIVER

CANAL

DUBROVY RYNOK

LAKE STAROTITAROVSKY

STRELKA

ANTI-TANK DITCH

LAK

KU

XXXXIX

KONRAD

EVENTS

1. 1 April 1943: 50.Infanterie-Division occupies the Katinka Stellung behind the Kurka River. The town of Kurchansky is heavily fortified.

2. 5 April: the German XXXXIX Gebirgskorps deploys Kampfgruppe Münchow to defend the coastline.

3. 10 April: 9th Army begins conducting frontal attacks in an effort to cross the river, but is repeatedly repulsed.

4. 1 May: the Soviet Azov Flotilla lands a battalion-size group on the Verbyanaya Spit, which begins an effort by 9th Army to skirt around the northern side of Lake Kurchansky.

5. 5 May: concerned about Soviet infiltration through the Lagoon sector, XXXXIX Gebirgskorps deploys Kampfgruppe Brücker to cover the gap between the coastal defences and 50.Infanterie-Division.

6. 6 May: elements of the Soviet 351st Rifle Division conduct a surprise attack and overrun one of the German platoon strongpoints on the northern side of Lake Kurchansky and attack another one. The 62nd Naval Rifle Brigade also infiltrates into this sector.

7. 7 May: XXXXIX Gebirgskorps commits its reserve, III./Grenadier-Regiment 121, which recaptures the strongpoint and temporarily pushes back some of the Soviet infiltration force.

8. 8–15 May: Soviet infiltrators continue to operate on the north side of Lake Kurchansky and even attempt to cross the lake at night. German Stukas, including that of Hans-Ulrich Rudel, are used to break up some of these infiltration attempts.

9. 22 May: XXXXIX Gebirgskorps makes another effort with Luftwaffe support to mop up infiltrators in the Lagoon sector, with partial success.

10. 21 June: 9th Army begins an effort to infiltrate a large force along the coastline, assembling on the Verbyanaya Spit. Their objective is Temryuk.

11. 3–5 July: Kampfgruppe Brücker blocks the Soviet infiltration and destroys hundreds of small boats with Flak guns and air strikes.

Note: Gridlines are shown at intervals of 5 km (3.1 miles)

N

9 KOROTEEV

KURKA RIVER

KALABATKA

SVETLYY PUT

KRASNY OKTYABR'

KORZHEVSKIY

FRONT LINE

THE STRUGGLE FOR TEMRYUK, 1 APRIL–5 JULY 1943

The German 50.Infanterie-Division was assigned to defend the so-called Lagoon sector along the Sea of Azov coast against the Soviet 9th Army, which launched repeated efforts to reach the port of Temryuk.

BATTLE OF ATTRITION, 26 MAY–22 AUGUST 1943

The battle of Moldavanskoye, 26 May–2 June

Once in command of the North Caucasus Front, Petrov attempted to implement Zhukov's instructions for the next set-piece battle. More artillery and tanks were brought forward and efforts were made to use engineer teams to locate and remove enemy minefields prior to the main attack. Petrov was able to amass a 3:1 local superiority in manpower, which was the recommended minimum for a successful attack against a fortified line. However, Petrov's actual battle plan was very similar to Maslennikov's last two offensives, with Grechko's 56th Army assigned to break through Gruppe Angelis' front north-east of Moldavanskoye, while the 37th Army made a supporting attack along the Adagum River. Although the 37th Army had built several trails across the marshes, it could not really mount a serious attack across the Adagum and instead assigned the 20th Mountain Rifle Division to harass the Romanian troops on the opposite bank. With Stavka on his back to not leave any armies idle, Petrov ordered Grechko to transfer Tikhonov's 11th Guards Rifle Corps to 37th Army so that it could conduct an attack south of the Adagum. Tikhonov was assigned to attack the town of Plavnenskiy and clear the north side of the Krymskaya–Varenikovskaya road.

Grechko was left with the 10th Guards Rifle Corps, 3rd Rifle Corps and four separate rifle divisions. He decided to make his main effort with Rubanyuk's 10th Guards Rifle Corps from Melehovsky against the Gorishny–Hill 121.4 sector, which was held by Vogel's 101.Jäger-Division. This was intended to be a powerful effort, with about 15,000 infantry and a brigade of tanks. Grechko assigned the 3rd Rifle Corps to several supporting attacks on Rubanyuk's left flank, including an effort to clear the Krymskaya–Moldavanskore road, held by 97.Jäger-Division. Although the North Caucasus Front enjoyed a large numerical superiority, the effort to amass three reinforced rifle corps and three tank units was dissipated by assigning one corps to 37th Army and giving too many missions to another corps. Only Rubanyuk's 10th Guards Rifle Corps was properly weighted to achieve its objectives, but Grechko had only the NKVD division as an exploitation force. Nor did Grechko's 56th Army employ *maskirovka* (deception) during its preparations for the offensive, so Gruppe Angelis was alerted to where the enemy intended to attack.

Gruppe Angelis' positions on the D-Stellung were similarly arranged to the defence used at Krymskaya, with Rupp's 97.Jäger-Division in the centre, Vogel's 101.Jäger-Division in the north and 9.Infanterie-Division in the south. However, one difference was the arrival of 79.Infanterie-Division in mid-May; the original division was destroyed at Stalingrad but a new division was formed from bits and pieces and sent to the Kuban. It would have made more sense for a reconstituted division like this to be sent to a quiet sector, but instead it was assigned to Gruppe Angelis and deployed in the Kiyevskoye–Plavnenskiye sector. Angelis also

Warfare in the Kuban was very reminiscent of World War I trench combat, with infantry focused on holding trench lines, with the one difference being minefields employed to slow attackers. The Blue Line was essentially a line of trenches, barbed wire and mines, supplemented by only a few bunkers made of timber and stone. (Nik Cornish at www.Stavka.org.uk)

integrated the Romanian 19th Infantry Division and 3rd Mountain Division into the two *Jäger-Divisionen*, providing them with additional troops. The German defence consisted of three to four rows of trenches, along with a few bunkers, behind minefields and supported by adequate artillery, but the only significant tactical reserve was Infanterie-Bataillon zbV 500 and a few independent *Pionier* units. Furthermore, Luftwaffe strength in the region was ebbing, as units were being transferred north in order to participate in the upcoming Operation *Zitadelle*. By mid-May, Fliegerkorps I had lost about half its fighters (Stab., II., III./Jagdgeschwader 3) and half its ground-attack aircraft (III./Sturzkampfgeschwader 77 and all of Sturzkampfgeschwader 2), leaving it with about 80 fighters and 70 ground-attack aircraft. In contrast, the 4th VA could commit 338 aircraft to support the new offensive, including 150 fighters and 104 Il-2 Sturmoviks.

At 0500hrs on 26 May, the Soviets began their artillery preparation against Gruppe Angelis, focusing on the sectors held by 101.Jäger-Division and 79.Infanterie-Division. At 0630hrs, 4th VA began its air attacks, first sending in a wave of 84 bombers, then a wave of 36 Il-2s, then a third wave with 49 Il-2s. Some of the Sturmoviks dropped smoke pots, to blind the German gunners just before the Soviet ground attack started. On the right, the 37th Army committed both Guards Rifle divisions from 11th Guards Rifle Corps and a tank brigade, which overwhelmed I./Grenadier-Regiment 226 (79.Infanterie-Division) and quickly captured Plavnenskiy. The battered German battalion retreated into the village of Borisovka but managed to repulse a follow-on attack by 11th Guards Rifle Corps and knock out 8 tanks. Nevertheless, 79.Infanterie-Division's left flank was pushed back and the division hastily refused the flank of the III./Grenadier-Regiment 226 and moved its reconnaissance battalion to reinforce the eastern defences of Kiyevskoye.

Rubanyuk's 10th Guards Rifle Corps attacked the centre of the line held by 101. Jäger-Division, which was defended by Kampfgruppe Busche (Jäger-Regiment 228) and Kampfgruppe Schury (Jäger-Regiment 229). Despite losses to mines and German defensive fire, the heavy smoke enabled the Soviet assault units to reach the German positions with enough combat power. The II./Jäger-Regiment 228 in Gorishny was hard hit by waves of Soviet infantry and tanks and forced to retreat, opening a gap in the centre of the German line. A supporting attack by 3rd Rifle Corps overran II./Jäger-Regiment 229 near Tambulovskiy, forcing Kampfgruppe Schury to retreat. Once Gorishny was taken and the German centre pierced,

German troops from Kampfgruppe Schury (Jäger-Regiment 229 from 101. Jäger-Division) were tasked with defending the marshlands along the Sea of Azov, north of Temryuk, against Soviet infiltration. The Germans had to use small boats to reach some positions that were virtually on small islands in a sea of reeds. This was a dangerous sector of the front, since the water precluded troops from digging in, making them more vulnerable to enemy artillery fire. (Author's collection)

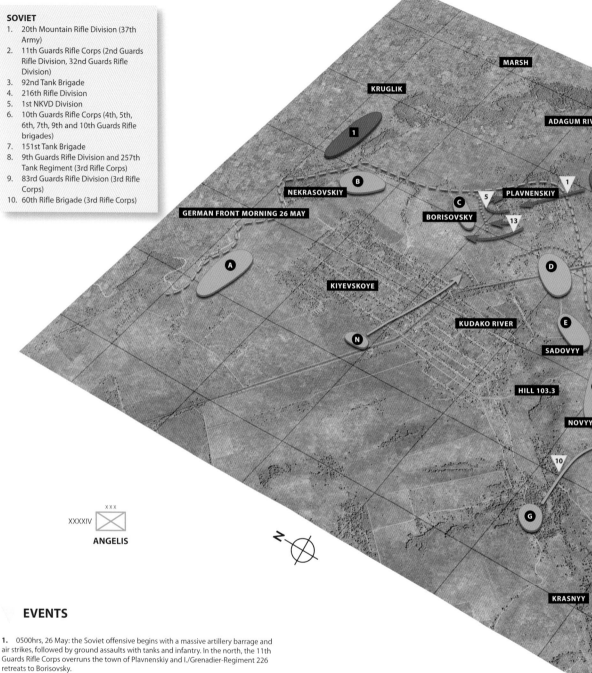

SOVIET

1. 20th Mountain Rifle Division (37th Army)
2. 11th Guards Rifle Corps (2nd Guards Rifle Division, 32nd Guards Rifle Division)
3. 92nd Tank Brigade
4. 216th Rifle Division
5. 1st NKVD Division
6. 10th Guards Rifle Corps (4th, 5th, 6th, 7th, 9th and 10th Guards Rifle brigades)
7. 151st Tank Brigade
8. 9th Guards Rifle Division and 257th Tank Regiment (3rd Rifle Corps)
9. 83rd Guards Rifle Division (3rd Rifle Corps)
10. 60th Rifle Brigade (3rd Rifle Corps)

MARSH

KRUGLIK

ADAGUM RIV

NEKRASOVSKIY

PLAVNENSKIY

GERMAN FRONT MORNING 26 MAY

BORISOVSKY

KIYEVSKOYE

KUDAKO RIVER

SADOVYY

HILL 103.3

NOVYY

XXXXIV ANGELIS

KRASNYY

EVENTS

1. 0500hrs, 26 May: the Soviet offensive begins with a massive artillery barrage and air strikes, followed by ground assaults with tanks and infantry. In the north, the 11th Guards Rifle Corps overruns the town of Plavnenskiy and I./Grenadier-Regiment 226 retreats to Borisovsky.

2. 0500–0600hrs: 10th Guards Rifle Corps smashes through Kampfgruppe Busche, which retreats to Hill 121.4.

3. 0500hrs: 9th Guards Rifle Division and tanks overrun II./Jäger-Regiment 229 and force Kampfgruppe Schury to retreat.

4. Morning: an attack by the rest of 3rd Rifle Corps on Hill 114.1 is repulsed by 97.Jäger-Division.

5. 0855hrs: 11th Guards Rifle Corps attacks I./Grenadier-Regiment 226 in Borisovsky but is repulsed.

6. The 10th Guards Rifle Corps pivots and storms Hill 121.4 before Kamfgruppe Busche can consolidate; Oberst Busche is badly wounded.

7. The rest of 10th Guards Rifle Corps overruns Gorishny and pursues Kampfgruppe Schury.

8. Kampfgruppe Schury hastily forms a new line between Podgorniy and Hill 95.

9. Late morning: 97.Jäger-Division shifts I./Jäger-Regiment 204 and some *Pioniere* to reinforce the division's left flank.

10. XXXXIV Armeekorps commits its reserves to rebuild a new front south of Kiyevskoye, including the Infanterie-Bataillon zbV 500, *Pioniere* and reconnaissance troops. By late afternoon, a hasty front has been established.

11. 0600hrs, 27 May: the Germans mount a three-pronged counterattack to restore their original HKL. Kampfguppe Liebmann (formerly Busche) recaptures Hill 121.4.

12. 0600hrs: Infanterie-Bataillon zbV 500 and Kampfgruppe Schury recapture part of Gorishny, but suffer heavy losses in the town.

13. Morning/afternoon 27 May: 11th Guards Rifle Corps mounts two major attacks to seize Borisovsky, but I./Grenadier-Regiment 226 repulses both attempts.

14. Rubanyuk's 10th Guards Rifle Corps commits its remaining troops and tanks and manages to push the Germans off Hill 121.4 again, but later loses this position to a night infiltration attack.

Note: Gridlines are shown at intervals of 2 km (1.24 miles)

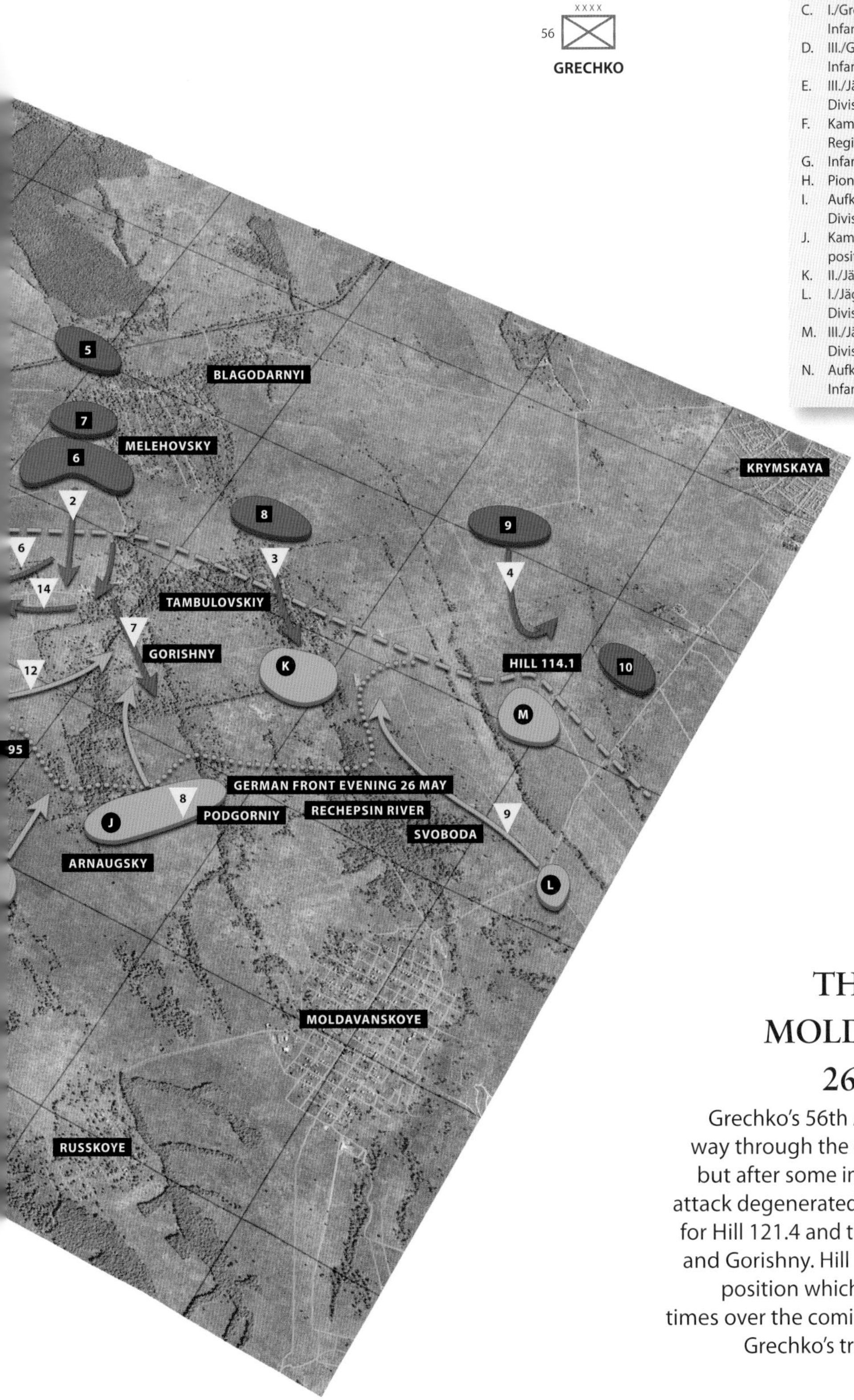

56
XXXX
GRECHKO

GERMAN
A. Battlegroup Marincescu (Romanian)
B. II/96th Infantry Regiment (Romanian)
C. I./Grenadier-Regiment 226 (79. Infanterie-Division)
D. III./Grenadier-Regiment 226 (79. Infanterie-Division)
E. III./Jäger-Regiment 228 (101.Jäger-Division)
F. Kampfgruppe Busche (I./Jäger-Regiment 228, II/95th Romanian)
G. Infanterie-Bataillon zbV 500
H. Pionier-Bataillon 46
I. Aufklärungs-Abteilung 97 (97.Jäger-Division)
J. Kampfgruppe Schury – second position (Jäger-Regiment 229)
K. II./Jäger-Regiment 229
L. I./Jäger-Regiment 204 (97.Jäger-Division)
M. III./Jäger-Regiment 204 (97.Jäger-Division)
N. Aufklärungs-Abteilung 179 (79. Infanterie-Division)

5
7
6
BLAGODARNYI
MELEHOVSKY
2
6
14
8
9
3
KRYMSKAYA
4
7
TAMBULOVSKIY
GORISHNY
12
K
HILL 114.1
10
95
M
8
J
GERMAN FRONT EVENING 26 MAY
PODGORNIY
RECHEPSIN RIVER
SVOBODA
9
ARNAUGSKY
L
MOLDAVANSKOYE

RUSSKOYE

THE BATTLE OF MOLDAVANSKOYE, 26–27 MAY 1943

Grechko's 56th Army tried to smash its way through the centre of the Blue Line, but after some initial success the Soviet attack degenerated into a slugging match for Hill 121.4 and the towns of Borisovsky and Gorishny. Hill 121.4 became a critical position which changed hands many times over the coming days, but ultimately Grechko's troops could not keep it.

Whenever the Germans lost a position, they were quick to mount counterattacks with their tactical reserves. Here, a soldier hurls a stick grenade at the enemy. The Germans proved masterful at scraping together ad hoc teams into effective assault groups. (Nik Cornish at www.Stavka.org.uk)

Rubanyuk pivoted some of his forces northwards and captured Hill 121.4 while the rest of his brigades pursued Kampfgruppe Schury. Oberst Karl Busche was mortally wounded in the fighting and his regiment was decimated. Kampfgruppe Schury was also mauled, losing a battalion commander. In the space of a couple of hours, Rubanyuk had advanced 3km, mauled several German battalions and secured a key tactical objective. This might have been the breakthrough that Petrov wanted, but Grechko slavishly stuck to the pre-battle plan and during the night he reoriented his forces to push south into the left flank of the intact 97.Jäger-Division, rather than west to smash through what was left of the battered 101.Jäger-Division. The lack of agility in the Soviet commanders and their inability to take advantage of fleeting opportunities was a recurring theme throughout the Kuban campaign.

Not much went right for the Soviets on either flank of the offensive. In the south, 97.Jäger-Division repulsed the 3rd Rifle Corps' under-resourced effort to seize Hill 114.1 and was able to transfer a couple of battalions to help Kampfgruppe Schury stabilize a new front between Podgorniy and Hill 95. In the north, the 11th Guards Rifle Corps remained stymied by the remnants of a single German battalion in Borisovka. On the first day of the offensive, 116 of 145 Soviet tanks committed were knocked out, but only 26 were recovered. The small number of remaining tanks were allowed to drift to the rear to refuel, then remained there. In addition, Fliegerkorps I appeared in strength over the battlefield in the late afternoon, which forced 4th VA to change from a ground support focus to defensive counter air. According to Grechko's post-war history, the Luftwaffe sent 600 bombers over the battlefield in a 20-minute period and this halted the Soviet offensive. However, Grechko's account is patently false both on the scale of the Luftwaffe intervention and its effects. Fliegerkorps I failed to stop Grechko's attack; it was the mines that disabled his armour and his own faulty battle plan.

During the afternoon and evening of 26 May, Group Angelis rushed its limited reserves to strengthen 101.Jäger-Division and create a new front. The Germans also planned to mount a multi-pronged counterattack the next morning to recover Gorishny and Hill 121.4. Around 0600hrs on 27 May, Kampfgruppe Liebmann (formerly Busche) attacked and recaptured Hill 121.4, while two other groups pushed into Gorishny. For a moment, Rubanyuk's 10th Guards Rifle Corps was caught off guard, but it quickly committed reserves into the fight and the small German assault groups were badly outnumbered. The Infanterie-Bataillon zbV 500 was decimated in the street fighting inside Gorishny and bodily ejected from the town. Then Rubanyuk committed his remaining troops and tanks and pushed the Germans off Hill 121.4 again. Fighting continued around the hill for the rest of the day, with the Germans recovering it with a night infiltration attack. In the north, the 11th Guards Rifle Corps launched a pre-dawn assault upon the I./Grenadier-Regiment 226 in Borisovka, but was repulsed again. The

German battalion was gutted and reduced to just 50 effectives, but it held off another attack and prevented Grechko's entire right wing from advancing. German losses were extremely heavy on 27 May, but the Soviet offensive had ground to a halt almost everywhere.

Soviet attacks continued on 28 and 29 May, but failed to achieve any progress against the hardened Axis defence. By 30 May, the exhausted Soviet divisions temporarily shifted to the defence to reorganize, although air battles continued overhead. During the late afternoon, Soviet Il-2s attacked the command post of 97.Jäger-Division near Moldavanskoye and Generalmajor Rupp was killed. Gruppe Angelis used the respite to prepare a major counterattack to finally eliminate the enemy salient created around Gorishny. In a post-battle report to Stavka, Petrov harshly criticized the performance of Soviet infantry and artillery in the offensive, particularly the inability to consolidate on an objective and establish communications with fire support before the inevitable German counterattack. He also criticized Soviet tactical-level command and control, but said nothing about Grechko's mistakes.

On the morning of 31 May, Kampfgruppe Gaza (I./Panzergrenadier-Regiment 66 and 12 PzKpfw IV tanks) and Kampfgruppe Polster (I., II./Panzergrenadier-Regiment 93, II./Panzer-Artillerie-Regiment 13 with 12 howitzers and Sturmgeschütz-Abteilung 191 with 21 StuG IIIs) attacked the Soviet positions around Gorishny. Yet despite hours of fighting, the Germans failed to restore their original HKL and were forced to call off their counterattack. Grechko's tired 56th Army responded with minor attacks on 1 and 2 June, but failed to seize any more ground. Petrov's first offensive ground to a halt after achieving only minor gains. Gruppe Angelis had been mauled, but held most of its ground. Overall, 17.Armee suffered over 9,500 casualties in May, including 3,743 dead or missing. Once the front quietened down, Generalmajor Ludwig Muller took over 97.Jäger-Division and prepared for the next round.

The vulnerable flanks, June–July

While the 56th Army tried to smash through the centre of the Axis front, the rest of the North Caucasus Front was engaged in desultory operations on the southern and northern flanks. In the south, the 47th Army had been withdrawn at the end of April and Leselidze's 18th Army was put in charge both of the forces in the Myskhako bridgehead and the sector just east of Novorossiysk. In theory, this meant that Leselidze could try to mount a coordinated attack upon Novorossiysk from both sides, but in reality his forces were spread too thinly for offensive action. He had the 16th Rifle Corps, 176th Rifle Division and the 81st Naval Rifle Brigade holding the bridgehead (about 20,000 combat troops) and the 20th Rifle Corps and 318th Rifle Division in the eastern sector (about 18,000 combat troops). At best, Leselidze could only commit a few brigades to any offensive, which was insufficient.

The German 73.Infanterie-Division had been holding its positions around Novorossiysk for nine months and its defence rested on two heavily fortified mountain ridges: the 500m Krymskaya-Dolgaya, 7km south of Neberdzhaevskaya, and the 588m Sakharnaya Golova, 3km north-east of the harbour. The Germans controlled the high ground, which was heavily wooded and marked by steep, rocky slopes. The Bogovo River running in

COUNTERATTACK! 28 MAY 1943 (PP. 72–73)

After repeated efforts to smash through the centre of the German Blue Line, the Soviet 56th Army shifted its main effort northwards in late May 1943 and tried to advance along the Kiyevskoye–Varenikovskaya road. The German 79.Infanterie-Division had been destroyed at Stalingrad in February but it was quickly reconstituted and sent to the Kuban in mid-May. Yet despite its ad hoc constitution, the new 79.Infanterie-Division proved very solid in the defence, even when attacked by masses of Soviet infantry and tanks on 27 May. The key to the German main line of defence in this sector proved to be the tiny village of Borisovka, just east of Kiyevskoye, held by I./Grenadier-Regiment 226. Relentless Soviet artillery bombardments and attacks decimated the German battalion, reducing it to just 83 men, but the village was held. After the battalion commander was badly wounded, Oberleutnant d. R. Karl-Will Lump, commander of 3.Kompanie, assumed command of the survivors.

On the morning of 28 May, the Soviet 32nd Guards Rifle Division (**1**) mounted an all-out attack, supported by tanks and artillery, which overran most of Borisovka. Lump (**2**) was wounded, and after most of their ammunition was exhausted, his men were forced to retreat into one corner of the village. However, German doctrine was always to counterattack before the enemy could consolidate on the objective and Lump managed to rally the last 50 survivors and lead them in a desperate effort to recover the village. The Germans surged forward, armed with entrenching tools, bayonets and rifle butts and caught the Soviet infantry by surprise. A frenzied, close-quarter melee ensued, while Lump managed to destroy a Soviet tank (**3**) with a magnetic mine. The fighting in Borisovka was vicious and typical of the infantry combat in the Kuban. Caught off balance by Lump's counterattack, the Soviets abandoned the village and retreated. Lump, who was wounded six times, was awarded the Ritterkreuz des Eisernen Kreuzes for his accomplishment in preventing an enemy breakthrough.

The harbour of Novorossiysk seen from the towering Sakharnaya Golova heights north-east of the city. Tsemes Bay is in the centre of the image and Mount Myskhako and the Malaya Zemlya beachhead are on the far side. On this side, 18th Army had to fight its way through the lower ground to reach the naval landing forces in the city, on the right. (Author's collection)

front of the German lines added additional difficulty for attackers. After repeated fruitless efforts to gain the heights in March 1943, Leselidze knew that he could not penetrate the German HKL and reach Novorossiysk with his own limited resources. Likewise, he had enough troops to hold the Myskhako bridgehead, but not enough to break out of it. By this point, the German 125.Infanterie-Division had built an iron ring around Myskhako, which could not be penetrated. However, the Romanian 6th Cavalry Division held the sector along the Black Sea and Leselidze thought its defence was not as solid. On 21 July, the Soviets mounted a brigade-size attack against the Romanian 5th Cavalry Regiment and succeeded in capturing a small hilltop position. With German help, the Romanians mounted several counterattacks, but failed to recover the lost ground. After this, the Germans decided to pull the Romanian 6th Cavalry Division out of the line and replaced it with troops from 4.Gebirgs-Division.

In the north, Stavka was extremely disappointed by the lack of progress by 9th Army and Kozlov was replaced by General-major Aleksei A. Grechkin on 17 June. The 9th Army staff had assembled a fleet of over 700 small boats, and Grechkin was ordered to mount an infiltration attack through the Lagoon area to reach the port of Temryuk. Grechkin decided to commit two rifle divisions to the operation, and by 21 June, the lead elements had succeeded in reaching the Verbyanaya Spit north-east of Temryuk without attracting too much attention. The idea was to continue further south along the coast at night and then suddenly land near the port. However, the Germans had detected the enemy infiltration and they reinforced Kampfgruppe Brücker with additional Flak guns. When the Soviet flotillas attempted to move along the coast, they were caught by searchlight beams and the Flak guns ripped the tiny boats to pieces. Now that the Germans knew that there was a large Soviet force on the Verbyanaya Spit, 50.Infanterie-Division blocked off the area on 3–4 July and called in the Luftwaffe to smash up the boat traffic. By 5 July, the 9th Army infiltration operation had turned into a costly fiasco, with over 700 boats lost and 630 troops captured. Although the German coastal defences had proved sound, Generalleutnant Friedrich Schmidt was not around to celebrate, since he was killed by a mine on 26 June.

Thus, the North Caucasus Front learned that the Axis flanks on both the Azov coast and Black Sea coast were held in force. In order to clear the Kuban, Petrov's forces were left with no choice but to pierce the enemy's heavily defended centre in another frontal assault.

Inertia and attrition, 7 June–22 August

After the failure to capture Moldavanskoye, the North Caucasus Front gradually transitioned to an active defence in early June. Stavka was aware that the Germans were preparing to conduct Operation *Zitadelle* soon and was unwilling to dispatch additional reinforcements to the Kuban to support more futile efforts in what was now a secondary theatre. Instead, Petrov was directed to reorganize his forces and conduct local operations to chip away at the enemy defences. The 37th Army was disbanded and its units assigned to the 9th and 56th armies. Grechko remained in command of the 56th Army and he remained as the primary Soviet tactical commander until the end of the Kuban campaign. Petrov's North Caucasus Front still had about 400,000 troops, but now in only three armies.

The air situation changed drastically in mid-June as both sides pulled out their best units and shifted them northwards to participate in the upcoming action around the Kursk salient. The 4th VA was directed to transfer a large number of aircraft to the 5th VA in the Steppe Front, including the 3rd Fighter Aviation Corps, a bomber division, a ground-attack division and several other regiments. General-leytenant of Aviation Konstantin A. Vershinin took over the reduced 4th VA, which was still numerically superior to the residual forces left with Fliegerkorps I.

The 17.Armee had suffered over 17,000 casualties in April and May, and since few replacements were available, it was clear that this rate of attrition could not be indefinitely sustained. German attention was focused on the Kursk salient and the Ukraine, not the Caucasus. Consequently, the Kuban had become an economy of force sector, where the OKH wanted to tie down the maximum amount of enemy forces with the least number of Axis divisions until Hitler eventually agreed to evacuate the bridgehead.

The liberation of Krasnodar by the 46th Army on the morning of 12 February 1943 was an ecstatic moment for the Soviet troops, but there was little else to celebrate until the Germans evacuated the Kuban eight months later. In July 1943, the North Caucasus Front conducted the first war crimes trial of World War II, focusing on crimes committed by SS-Einsatzgruppe D in the Krasnodar area in 1942 and 1943. Eight local men who served as auxiliaries in the SS unit were tried and publicly hanged in Krasnodar on 18 July 1943. This show trial set the standard for later Soviet tribunals against German war criminals. (Author's collection)

Nevertheless, the OKH was directed to send a few reinforcements during the summer, including 98.Infanterie-Division and a Romanian tank battalion. On 1 July, 98.Infanterie-Division began taking over the front-line positions of the much-depleted 101.Jäger-Division near Kiyevskoye, allowing that veteran formation to go into reserve to rest.

Hitler was still adamant about holding the Kuban bridgehead simply for prestige reasons, but he had grown tired of Ruoff's uninspired leadership. On 24 June, General der Pioniere Erwin Jänecke replaced Ruoff as commander of 17.Armee; Ruoff was sent off to virtual retirement in the Führer-Reserve. Jänecke was a survivor of Stalingrad and hardly an improvement since he was not an energetic commander either, but Hitler thought a new face at the top would be good.

On 28 June, Stavka Directive No. 30143 to the North Caucasus Front outlined the basic concept for a new offensive to liberate the Kuban, which entailed massing overwhelming force opposite Gruppe Angelis' positions around the villages of Gorishchny and Novyy. At this point, Soviet operational planning in the Kuban was bankrupt of imagination and a front comprising 400,000 troops had reduced its focus to seizing just a few kilometres of terrain. Despite suffering heavy losses to capture and hold the Malaya Zemlya, Petrov could not figure out how to make use of it. Instead, Petrov intended to just keep battering against the German Blue Line, content to fight a battle of attrition.

The long-awaited German offensive against the Kursk salient, Operation *Zitadelle*, began on 5 July, and von Manstein's Heeresgruppe Süd made good progress in the first few days, penetrating the second Soviet defensive line. Both LII Armeekorps headquarters and 198.Infanterie-Division, which had been withdrawn from the Kuban, participated in the offensive. However, Soviet resistance forced von Manstein to fight a battle of attrition, which gradually sapped Heeresgruppe Süd's offensive power. On 13 July, Hitler ordered *Zitadelle* suspended. It was now evident that Germany had permanently lost the initiative in the East.

Three days later, Petrov began the fourth Soviet offensive to liberate the Kuban with another massive artillery barrage at 0400hrs. However, he initially attacked with just the 10th Guards Rifle Corps and 11th Guards Rifle Corps in a 7km-wide sector against the boundary between 97.Jäger-Division and 98.Infanterie-Division. The fighting quickly focused on just three small hills – Hill 95, Hill 114.1 and Hill 121.4 – located between Novyy and Gorishny, which had been contested so much in May. Petrov hoped to secure all three hills before beginning the main offensive, but the limited attack sector enabled Gruppe Angelis to channel its tactical reserves into this area. Hauptmann Alfred Müller's Sturmgeschütz-Abteilung 191 methodically picked off the Soviet tanks that tried to move forward to support the Soviet infantry. The German defence held, so Petrov kept attacking, day after day. In a pointless battle reminiscent of Passchendaele, the 56th Army continued its daily offensive pushes, which gained virtually no ground. Although 98.Infanterie-Division suffered 1,767 casualties in 12 days of fighting, Petrov failed to capture any of the three hills.

On 22 July, Petrov ordered the rest of the 56th Army to join the offensive, which included the 3rd, 10th and 16th Rifle Corps – a total of eight more rifle divisions and about 100 tanks. While this increased the length of German front under attack, the Soviet attacks were not well coordinated. One of

Soviet naval infantry, armed with anti-tank rifles and sub-machine guns, in the Malaya Zemlya lodgement. What started as a company-size beachhead eventually grew to an army-size lodgement by spring 1943. Despite repeated efforts, the Germans could not eliminate this Soviet position and it drew several divisions away from the main front in the Kuban. However, holding the Malaya Zemlya cost the Soviets tens of thousands of casualties. (Author's collection)

the most powerful assaults occurred on 26 July, when Grenadier-Regiment 282 from 98.Infanterie-Division was attacked by waves of infantry and 80 tanks. The fighting lasted for hours and was intense, with hand-to-hand combat in some places. Nevertheless, the German HKL held and the Soviet offensive ebbed. When checked, Petrov would take a few days to regroup and then begin attacking again. Even though it was only a supporting attack, the 3rd Rifle Corps managed to push back a Romanian battalion on Gruppe Angelis' right flank, but the penetration was quickly sealed off by German reserves.

The final phase of this unimaginative offensive occurred between 7 and 12 August, with the 11th Guards Rifle Corps trying to stove in 97.Jäger-Division's right flank. Briefly, the 56th Army managed to achieve some local penetrations before German reserves restored their original HKL with sharp counterattacks. By 12 August, the fourth Soviet offensive had failed and the next day Stavka concurred. Petrov's two offensives had cost the North Caucasus Front over 161,000 casualties, or 40 per cent of its manpower. The 17.Armee suffered over 22,000 casualties in this period, meaning that it inflicted better than 7:1 losses on the enemy. Even Stavka realized that further large-scale offensives in this area were a waste of resources. Consequently, on 22 August Stavka ordered the North Caucasus Front to transfer seven of its rifle divisions to the Stavka Reserves and the front was to transition to a defensive posture; the North Caucasus Front had been fought to a standstill and Stavka wanted to use its troops elsewhere.

THE GERMAN EVACUATION OF THE KUBAN, 1 SEPTEMBER–9 OCTOBER 1943

The Novorossiysk landing operation, 10–14 September

While the Red Army's repeated efforts to break through 17.Armee's front had failed, the prospects facing the North Caucasus Front gradually improved due to the deteriorating situation of Heeresgruppe Süd after the failure of Operation *Zitadelle*. On 3 August, the Soviet Voronezh and Steppe fronts began their counter-offensive, known as Operation *Rumyantsev*, which inflicted grievous damage upon von Manstein's forces. By 23 August, the Red Army had liberated Kharkov and Heeresgruppe Sud lacked the reserves to stop the relentless Soviet hammer blows. With the entire German position in the eastern Ukraine at risk, von Manstein pleaded with the OKH to evacuate the Kuban bridgehead so that 17.Armee could be used to reinforce his army group. Generalfeldmarschall Ewald von Kleist, commander of Heeresgruppe A, which controlled 17.Armee, also pushed for evacuating the Kuban. Initially, the OKH only agreed to the withdrawal of 13.Panzer-Division from the Kuban, but this was just the beginning. By the end of August, Hitler was finally convinced that 17.Armee was better employed elsewhere. On the afternoon of 3 September, Hitler finally changed his mind and agreed to evacuate the Kuban bridgehead. The next day, von Kleist was told to begin preparations to evacuate the Kuban bridgehead within a matter of days. In fact, von Kleist's staff had been quietly working on contingency evacuation plans for some time and were able to quickly pull together a plan known as *Brunhild* for a phased withdrawal from the Kuban, to be completed within five weeks. For the first time in World War II, the Germans were going to move an entire army by sea.

Soviet infantrymen fighting on a wooded slope, probably near Novorossiysk. The city had been fought over for a year and was blasted into rubble. By the time it was liberated on 16 September 1943, the city which had a pre-war population of 96,000 was reduced to only 1,200 civilians. (Author's collection)

Although Petrov was not yet aware of the impending withdrawal of 17.Armee, he ordered his 9th, 18th and 56th armies to conduct local fixing attacks to try and prevent the Germans from withdrawing any units to send to Heeresgruppe Süd. Beginning on 1 September, the Soviets began probing attacks in up to regimental strength, looking for weak spots, but found none. On 6 September, 17.Armee was told to transfer 125.Infanterie-Division to Heeresgruppe Süd immediately, even though the evacuation had not yet begun. The Axis could not completely conceal that they were pulling units out of the Kuban and Petrov decided to implement more aggressive measures.

A naval assault force was assembled in Gelendzhik under the command of Rear-Admiral Georgy Kholostyakov. The landing force consisted of 8,935 troops from Polkovnik Aleksei S. Potapov's 255th Naval Rifle Brigade (two battalions), the 1339th Rifle Regiment (two battalions), the 290th NKVD Regiment and the 393rd Independent Naval Infantry Battalion, who were loaded onto 129 small craft. The escort force consisted of 25 G-5-type torpedo cutters. The concept was to attempt a coup de main-type assault into the inner harbour of Novorossiysk to seize multiple bridgeheads while the 18th Army tried to break out of the Malaya Zemlya lodgement. Another force, comprising the 318th Rifle Division, part of the 55th Guards Rifle Division and eight tanks, would assault into the eastern side of Novorossiysk, near the Proletary Cement Factory.

The German V Armeekorps, now under General der Infanterie Karl Allmendinger, still had 4.Gebirgs-Division containing the 20th Rifle Corps in the Malaya Zemlya, while 73.Infanterie-Division defended the high ground on the eastern approaches to Novorossiysk. Even though the Kriegsmarine had never operated from Novorossiysk, it was put in charge of harbour defence. Kapitänleutnant Hans Hossfeld had two companies of naval infantry to guard the harbour, supplemented by numerous Flak positions, while the harbour entrance was barred by nets and booms, plus mines. In order to block landing craft, the Germans installed a line of sharpened wooden stakes 20–50m from the water's edge.

A Soviet 82mm mortar team prepares to support an attack on an enemy position. The Red Army employed mortars in great numbers and they were useful for both smoke to conceal assault troops and high-explosive to suppress trenches. (Courtesy of the Central Museum of the Armed Forces, Moscow via Stavka)

Rear-Admiral Kholostyakov assembled his assault force inside Tsemes Bay by 2200hrs on 10 September; the time was chosen because the moon had set – thereby reducing illumination. Bombers from the VVS-ChF began attacking enemy coastal positions at this point, which helped to cover the noise of the approaching naval flotilla and to divert the enemy's attention. Kapitan 2nd Rank Viktor T. Protsenko led a special assault group of seven torpedo cutters and four other boats, which attacked the enemy's outer harbour defences at 0244hrs. At the same time, over 800 guns, mortars and rocket launchers from the eastern side of the bay began shelling the German coastal positions. Soon, the harbour area was covered with smoke. Although the Germans opened fire, Protsenko's squadron was able to penetrate the boom with torpedoes and explosives, and at 0300hrs, he signalled, 'The entrance to the port is open!' Two more groups of torpedo cutters immediately raced into the harbour to try to suppress the German defences with heavy machine-gun fire. German return fire was ferocious, but the first landing group with 84 boats pressed through the torrent and began landing the troops of the 255th Naval Infantry Brigade on the western side of the harbour. Shortly thereafter, Leytenant Vasily A. Botylev's 393rd Independent Naval Infantry Battalion landed directly on the central pier near the rail yard, while the 1339th Naval Infantry Regiment landed 1,000 troops on the eastern mole. Losses were heavy but more than half of the assault force made it ashore. At least two torpedo cutters and three MO-IV type patrol boats were sunk and many more damaged. Furthermore, none of the Soviet beachheads were connected to each other and once the sun came up, it would be virtually impossible for boat traffic to run the gauntlet into the harbour and reach the beaches.

Unfortunately, the Soviet ground operation to support the landing did not go according to schedule. The effort by the 20th Rifle Corps to break out of the Malaya Zemlya and push forward towards the beachheads held by the 255th Naval Infantry Brigade was easily frustrated by the immoveable defence of Oberst Ludwig Hörl's Gebirgsjäger-Regiment 91. Likewise, attacks by the 318th Rifle Division made only minor gains against the 73.Infanterie-Division positions on the east side of Novorossiysk. Although the Soviets still had strong air and artillery assets available to support the landing force, they could not break through to the isolated naval infantrymen. Botylev's battalion was in the greatest danger, being spread out in three separate locations, near the old passenger terminal in central Novorossiysk. Fortunately, the 23-year-old Botylev was no rookie; he had fought in the Crimea in 1942 and had landed with Kunikov in February 1943. Now he was in command of a battalion and armed to the teeth with machine guns, light mortars and anti-tank rifles.

Once it was clear that Soviet ground operations to link up with the landing force had failed, V Armeekorps began to shift troops into Novorossiysk to begin counterattacks. Two battalions of 4.Gebirgsjäger-Division, supported by *Pioniere* and artillery, quickly massed against Potapov's 255th Naval Rifle Battalion on the western side of the harbour and hit it hard. Potapov's brigade was broken into pieces and virtually destroyed. However, only the Romanian 20th Mountain Battalion could be sent to deal with Botylev's foothold in the city centre and the Romanian battalion commander was one of the early casualties. On 11 September, the Axis continued their counterattacks into the city and nearly crushed the 1339th Naval Infantry Regiment on the eastern side of the harbour, but it just managed to hold on until the 318th Rifle Division succeeded in landing reinforcements from the 1337th Rifle Regiment. Petrov also gave Leselidze the rest of the 55th Guards Rifle Division and the 5th Guards Tank Brigade to invigorate the effort to reach the beleaguered landing troops.

On the morning of 12 September, the 18th Army began pushing into the eastern suburbs of Novorossiysk. By 13 October, a ground link had been established with the 1337th and 1339th Rifle regiments and much of the eastern side of the city was in Soviet hands. At the same time, the German position on Sakharnaya Golova overlooking the city had been outflanked and 73.Infanterie-Division was forced backwards. Anticipating an evacuation order, V Armeekorps shifted to the defence and merely tried to delay the Soviet advance for as long as possible.

A Gebirgsjäger from 4.Gebirgsjäger Division stands on watch in a shallow trench in the Kuban, probably near the Malaya Zemlya beachhead, in the summer of 1943. After failing to crush the Soviet beachhead, 4.Gebirgsjäger Division spent the rest of the campaign trying to prevent the Soviet 18th Army from breaking out. Given that the soldier is standing upright and the trench is not very deep, this is likely a reserve position. (Author's collection)

Evacuation of the Kuban, 15 September–9 October 1943

The German intent was for 17.Armee to conduct a phased withdrawal from its current positions back into the Taman Peninsula, while the Kriegsmarine began the evacuation from the port of Anapa and other locations along the coast. However, the Soviets were aware of the impending German withdrawal and attacked all along the line in order to fix the enemy in place. On 15 September, 56th Army launched a division-size attack supported by tanks against 79.Infanterie-Division near Kiyevskoye, but was repulsed by strong German artillery fire. However, 18th Army had more success and was able to capture some of the high ground overlooking Novorossiysk. Around 1900hrs on 15 September, the 9., 79. and 98.Infanterie-Division and 97.Jäger-Division began pulling back to the Siegfried Stellung and 73.Infanterie-Division abandoned Novorossiysk. The Romanian 4th Mountain Division quietly withdrew from its positions around the Myskhako bridgehead without being noticed and retreated westwards. The next morning, 18th Army advanced unopposed into Novorossiysk and linked up with the remaining troops of the landing force, including Botylev's battalion, which had been surrounded for six days. Botylev was awarded a well-earned Hero of the Soviet Union for his exemplary leadership.

Phased withdrawal, 15 September–9 October

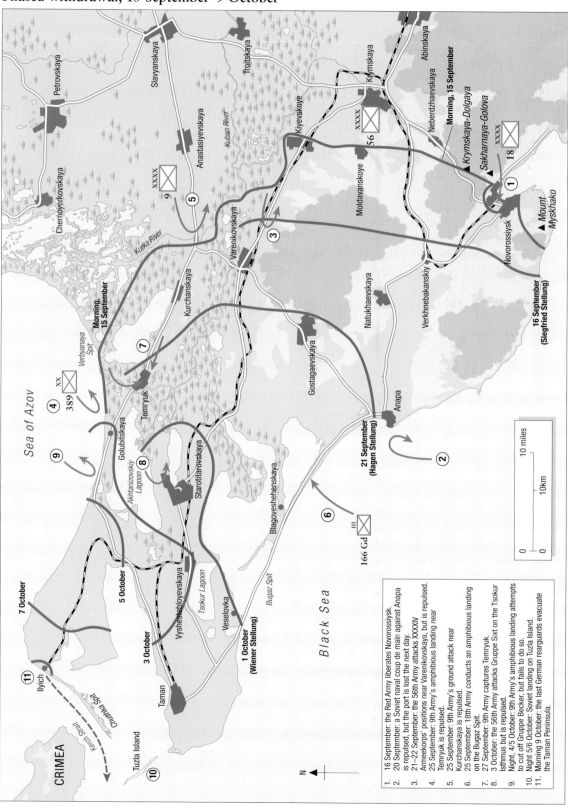

1. 16 September: the Red Army liberates Novorossiysk.
2. 20 September: a Soviet naval coup de main against Anapa is repulsed, but the port is lost the next day.
3. 21–22 September: the 56th Army attacks XXXIV Armeekorps' positions near Varenikovskaya, but is repulsed.
4. 25 September: 9th Army's amphibious landing near Temryuk is repulsed.
5. 25 September: 9th Army's ground attack near Kurchanskaya is repulsed.
6. 25 September: 18th Army conducts an amphibious landing on the Bugaz Spit.
7. 27 September: 9th Army captures Temryuk.
8. 3 October: the 56th Army attacks Gruppe Sixt on the Tsokur Isthmus but is repulsed.
9. Night, 4/5 October: 9th Army's amphibious landing attempts to cut off Gruppe Becker, but fails to do so.
10. Night 5/6 October: Soviet landing on Tuzla Island.
11. Morning 9 October: the last German rearguards evacuate the Taman Peninsula.

Now that the Germans were retreating, Petrov intended to keep the pressure on them and the 56th Army repeatedly attacked the rearguards of XXXXIV Armeekorps. The 18th Army also put heavy pressure on the retreating 4.Gebirgs-Division, which turned to fight just west of Novorossiysk. Heavy fighting occurred on both 16 and 17 September, but Petrov's pursuit failed to pin any German units. On 18 September, XXXXIX Gebirgskorps also began to withdraw from its positions north of the Kuban River. The Soviets used tanks in the pursuit, but only in small numbers – which the German Panzerjägers could handle. The Germans had also prepared fall-back positions along their line of retreat, which helped to slow the Soviet pursuit. Nevertheless, 18th Army reached the outskirts of Anapa on 20 September and attacked 4.Gebirgsjäger-Division and the Romanian 19th Infantry Division. Here, the Soviets had more luck and penetrated the city the next morning. A flotilla of six Soviet torpedo cutters attempted to land naval infantry in Anapa's harbour but were repulsed by Romanian mountain troops. Nevertheless, Anapa was yielded and V Armeekorps settled into positions just west of the city. By the end of 21 September, all of 17.Armee's major units had reached the Hagen Stellung; in this position the Axis front line was narrowed from the previous 90km-wide front to a 60km-wide one.

On 21 and 22 September, 56th Army pounded the XXXXIV Armeekorps positions near Varenikovskaya, but were repulsed by assault guns. On 23 September, 17.Armee shortened its right flank by pulling V Armeekorps back about 10–12km to the Rüdiger Stellung. Part of 50.Infanterie-Division, which was designated as Gruppe Sixt after Generalleutnant Friedrich Sixt, began pulling back to the Taman Peninsula to organize the final positions. The Soviets conducted strong probing

German troops evacuating from the Kuban. Units were able to cross the Kerch Strait in good order and with all their vehicles. Moving an entire army by sea was a major accomplishment for the Axis. (Nik Cornish at www.Stavka.org.uk)

A pair of German MFP landing craft crossing the Kerch Strait at dusk. The MFPs were very versatile craft and several were converted into Flak ships, armed with multiple 2cm and 3.7cm anti-aircraft guns, to keep marauding Soviet fighter-bombers away. Without regular runs by convoys of MFPs, 17.Armee could not have held the Kuban bridgehead. (Süddeutsche Zeitung, 00404159)

attacks all along the front of 24 September, without success.

Petrov increased the pressure by mounting two amphibious operations on the night of 25 September. The first was an attempt by a reinforced battalion from the 389th Rifle Division, which attempted to land near Temryuk. At the same time, the 9th Army mounted a major attack near Kurchanskaya from the east. However, the 50. and 370. Infanterie-Division were able to repulse the ground assault and then destroy the Soviet landing force. By this point, the German evacuation operation was proceeding in earnest and both V Armeekorps and XXXXIV Armeekorps were withdrawn to the Crimea. Eight Axis divisions (9., 73., 79. and 125.Infanterie-Division, 101.Jäger-Division, and the Romanian 10th Infantry, 9th Cavalry and 1st Mountain divisions) were queuing to withdraw across the Kerch Strait as transport resources allowed. Konrad's XXXXIX Gebirgskorps was assigned to fight the rear-guard action with six divisions (the 50., 98. and 370.Infanterie-Division, 97.Jäger-Division, 4.Gebirgs-Division and the Romanian 19th Infantry Division).

The five Romanian divisions had begun evacuating on 21 September, and by 28 September, all but the 19th Infantry Division had withdrawn to the Crimea. The 19th Infantry was deployed on the south side of the Taman Peninsula and performed well when attacked by Soviet tanks and infantry on 22 and 23 September. Romanian anti-tank gunners succeeded in knocking out 21 Soviet tanks, then continued their withdrawal.

Petrov's second amphibious operation occurred on the Black Sea coast, just west of Blagoveshchenskaya, with about 800 troops from the 166th Guards Rifle Regiment (55th Guards Rifle Division) landing on the Bugaz Spit. This was a foolish move since the Soviet regiment had landed on a 100m-wide strip of sand that was completely devoid of cover and the Romanian 9th Cavalry Division still occupied the town of Blagoveshchenskaya that controlled the eastern exit off the spit as well as Veselovka on the western end. The Soviet landing force was nicely bottled up and could be pounded with artillery and bombed by Stukas. The Romanian cavalry also mounted a counterattack, supported by a few tanks, which inflicted losses on the landing force. Amazingly, the Soviets kept landing more troops on this vulnerable position and the VVS-ChF provided strong air support. Nevertheless, Konrad was able to isolate this landing force and hold his positions for a week, while the rest of 17.Armee withdrew across the Kerch Strait.

Meanwhile, 9th Army continued to try to reach Temryuk, but the waterlogged terrain in the area prevented the use of tanks and made it difficult to bring heavy artillery forward. Instead, 9th Army continued small-scale infantry attacks through the marshes, supported by the Azov Flotilla's gunboats and the 4th VA. Despite the failure of the first landing near Temryuk, 9th Army tried again and managed to gain a toehold on the

coast which the Germans could not evict. After two days of heavy fighting, the Germans finally abandoned Temryuk on 27 September. Two days later, XXXXIX Gebirgskorps began pulling back to the Vienna Stellung, where the terrain greatly favoured the defence. Three large lagoons lay along the front line, limiting Soviet attacks to just three very narrow corridors. Although all three Soviet armies were pushing into the Taman Peninsula, there was only enough space to deploy a few units on-line and most of Petrov's forces were no longer actively involved in the pursuit phase.

Konrad only held the Vienna Stellung for a few days, then pulled back to the even shorter Bucharest Stellung on the night of 2/3 October. The lower Taman Peninsula was abandoned to the 18th Army without a fight. In the centre, the 56th Army attacked Gruppe Sixt on 3 October across the narrow 8km-wide isthmus between the Tsokur and Akhtanizovskiy lagoons and was repulsed. The next night, the Germans pulled back a bit further but were hit by a very strong attack on 4 October. The 56th Army committed its armour, hoping to crash through the retreating Germans, but the Sturmgeschütz-Abteilung 191 put teeth in the rear-guard and about 30 Soviet tanks were knocked out. Gruppe Becker was still located on the Sea of Azov coast near Golubitskaya and the Soviet 9th Army made another amphibious landing in an effort to cut it off, but the effort failed. On the night of 5 October, the Germans pulled back to the Berlin Stellung, which had only a 16km-wide front. The last Romanian troops left the Kuban on the night of 5 October.

Late on 6 October, Konrad and Jänecke pulled their headquarters back to Ilyich on the Kerch Strait and the 50. and 370.Infanterie-Division crossed over to the Crimea. The final German rear-guard actions in the Kuban were conducted by 4.Gebirgsjäger-Division and 97.Jäger-Division on 7 and 8 October. Although the Soviets kept attacking every day with both infantry and armour, the Luftwaffe played a vital role in disrupting these efforts. The Germans also had positioned artillery near Kerch which could fire across the strait to cover the withdrawal. Finally, the German rear-guards pulled into a tight perimeter around Ilyich on the night of 8/9 October and the last unit to leave was Gebirgsjäger-Regiment 13, which embarked at 0100hrs on

A German Schnellboot (S-boat) operating in the Black Sea. Although the Kriegsmarine presence in this region was tiny, it proved decisive in sustaining 17.Armee's sea lines of communications and continuously fending off the Black Sea Fleet. (Nik Cornish at www.Stavka.org.uk)

9 October. The next morning, the Soviet troops completed their liberation of the last piece of the Kuban.

Operation Brunhild, 15 September–9 October

The Kriegsmarine's ability to evacuate over 227,000 Axis troops and all their equipment from the Kuban in a little over three weeks – despite intense enemy air and naval attacks – was a remarkable achievement. In anticipation of *Brunhild*, the Germans were able to assemble almost 30 MFPs and a number of other small craft from Pionier-Landungs-Bataillon 86 in the Kerch area to conduct the evacuation and could begin as soon as authorization was provided. The MFPs, which were heavily armed with 2cm and 3.7cm Flak guns, usually moved across the Kerch Strait in small groups of two to three barges; it took five hours to reach the port of Anapa but just over an hour to reach Taman. This is where the German investment in amphibious technology for the proposed invasion of England in 1940 – Operation *Sea Lion* – really paid off, since the MFPs could operate from very rudimentary facilities and could load troops and vehicles directly off beaches. A single small convoy could move the bulk of a German battalion across the Kerch Strait. Even the Royal Romanian Navy was persuaded to deploy some of its ships to the region to assist in evacuating its troops from the Kuban. In order to discourage Soviet interference with the daily convoys, the Kriegsmarine laid defensive minefields near the Kerch Strait and deployed most of their available S-boats and R-boats and a flotilla of sub-chasers in the area.

Throughout September 1943, the Black Sea Fleet and its VVS-ChF made only half-hearted efforts to interfere with the German evacuation. Oddly, the aircraft best suited to interdicting the enemy convoys – the A-20C Bostons and Il-4s – were sent to mine the mouth of the Danube River but dropped only four mines in the Kerch Strait. Vice-Admiral Lev Vladimirsky, the new commander of the Black Sea Fleet, was reluctant to risk his remaining operational big ships – three cruisers and six destroyers – and instead chose to rely upon light forces and his naval air units. The Black Sea Fleet regularly sent torpedo cutters and submarines to try to intercept German convoys near Kerch, but they achieved very little. Patrols occurred at night and, without surface search radar, it was difficult for the Soviet boats to locate enemy coastal shipping.

On 26 September, four MO-IV patrol boats intercepted two MFPs, but the Soviets came off worse in the gun duel with one boat badly damaged. Two days later, four German S-boats caught a group of Soviet minesweepers

The Germans and Romanians were forced to deploy considerable numbers of troops all along the Kuban coast due to repeated efforts by the Soviets to land troops behind the front. Here, two soldiers man a rifle pit on the coast. At night, exposed positions like this could easily be overrun by a sudden landing. (Nik Cornish at www.Stavka.org.uk)

and sank two of them. On 29 September, two torpedo cutters engaged two R-boats and were also driven off with damage. The Soviet light craft lacked the speed and firepower of their German opponents and could not gain even momentary control over the Kerch Strait area. Soviet light craft did manage to mine some of the waters off the Taman Peninsula, which occasionally sank or damaged enemy vessels. However, the Black Sea Fleet had only limited numbers of older contact mines available and enemy coastal batteries prevented them from mining the main shipping lane inside the Kerch Strait.

General-major Vasily V. Ermachenkov's VVS-ChF had three primary anti-shipping units: the Pe-2s of 40 Bomber Aviation Regiment-VMF, the Il-4s of 5th Guards Mine-Torpedo Aviation Regiment and the Bostons of 36th Mine-Torpedo Aviation Regiment, along with two regiments of Il-2 Sturmoviks. If Ermachenkov had massed his available aircraft against German shipping, he might have inflicted considerable damage. Instead, he spread his aircraft across a variety of missions and targets, including raids on the ports of Sevastopol and Kerch. On the afternoon of 28 September, he sent seven A-20C torpedo bombers from 36th Mine-Torpedo Aviation Regiment on a 1,500km round-trip raid from Gelendzhik to Constanta in Romania, which cost him several of his best crews. Ermachenkov's naval aircraft did have some success, sinking the *S-46* and later the *R-30* off the Crimea. However, the VVS-ChF aircraft tended to carry light bomb loads and drop them from too high, which limited their ability to hit fast-moving small craft. German defences in the Kerch Strait were reinforced with additional Flak batteries and the Freya early warning radar in the Crimea was used to detect incoming raids and vector fighters to intercept. Soviet naval air operations over the Kerch Strait fell far short of what was needed, but Petrov kept 4th VA supporting his futile ground assaults.

Lacking serious enemy opposition, the German landing flotillas were able to move back and forth across the Kerch Strait at will, slowly evacuating 17.Armee piece by piece. The 1.Schnellbootsflotille was positioned near the Taman Peninsula each night, to prevent the Soviets from making an amphibious end-run behind German lines. As Konrad's rearguards pulled back into the Taman Peninsula, the Kriegsmarine prepared for Operation *Wiking* – the evacuation of the final elements.

By early October, Vice-Admiral Vladimirsky finally realized that 17.Armee was escaping virtually intact from the Kuban and decided to be more aggressive. He assembled a surface action group consisting of the Flotilla Leader Kharkov and the destroyers *Bezposhchadny* and *Sposobnyi* to intercept the German *Wiking* convoys. Vladimirsky also assigned a flotilla of eight torpedo cutters to support the operation and VVS-ChF aircraft for air cover. Since the Luftwaffe presence in the region was sharply reduced since June, he apparently did not regard enemy airpower as a serious threat. At 2030hrs on 5 October, the surface action group left Tuapse and headed towards the Crimea, with the intent of intercepting the *Wiking* convoys before they reached Feodosiya. Just before dawn on 6 October, the destroyers were spotted by a German reconnaissance aircraft and then stumbled upon three S-boats eight miles off Feodosiya. After firing their torpedoes – all of which missed – the German S-boats beat a hasty retreat. It was clear that surprise was lost and the enemy convoys were unlikely to be caught now, but amazingly the flotilla leader decided to carry on with his secondary mission, which was to bombard the port of Yalta. The *Kharkov* was sent on its own to conduct a 16-minute bombardment of the port, which was completed by 0715hrs. By 0800hrs, all three destroyers had re-formed and were heading back to Tuapse. Three VVS-ChF Pe-2 bombers were overhead to provide air cover.

Once the sun came up, the Luftwaffe sent reconnaissance aircraft out to look for the retreating Soviet destroyers and alerted the III./Sturzkampfgeschwader 3 stationed near Kerch. Although the VVS-ChF Pe-2s managed to shoot down a reconnaissance aircraft, it managed to report the position of the task force and around 0900hrs eight Ju-87 Stukas, two Bf-109Gs and two Fw-190s appeared. While the Bf-109s drove off the Pe-2s, the Stukas hit *Kharkov* with three 250kg bombs and crippled her. Rather than scuttling the *Kharkov*, the flotilla commander decided to take her in tow, which slowed the whole group down to 6–8 knots. At 1150hrs, another group of Stukas appeared and this time the *Bezposhchadny* was badly damaged. A third attack occurred at 1413hrs and *Bezposhchadny* broke in half and sank after four more bomb hits. The flotilla was still more than 100 miles from Gelendzhik and air cover from the VVS-ChF remained inadequate, so the Stukas piled on, sinking the *Kharkov* at 1537hrs. Finally, the *Sposobnyi* was sunk at 1835hrs. Altogether, 716 of the 903 crewmen on the three warships were lost. Stalin was shocked by the loss of three modern destroyers and forbade Vladimirsky from risking his big ships any more.

Consequently, the Kriegsmarine was able to complete the evacuation of the Kuban with minimal losses. Three MFPs were lost on mines off the Taman Peninsula, but none were loaded when they sank. When operations *Brunhild* and *Wiking* were completed, the Kriegsmarine had evacuated a total of 227,494 Axis soldiers (177,355 German), 74 tanks and assault guns, 21,230 trucks, 1,815 guns, 73,000 horses and 115,477 tons of supplies from the Kuban bridgehead to the Crimea. Of the nine German divisions evacuated from the Kuban bridgehead, seven were rushed to reinforce Heeresgruppe Süd's 6.Armee at Melitopol, while two were left to rebuild in the Crimea. All the Romanian divisions were left to guard the coast of the Crimea.

AFTERMATH

The Kuban campaign was unnecessary, but both Hitler and Stalin opted to commit large forces to a region that was no longer relevant to their overall strategic objectives. Once the German Army in Russia was gutted by the disaster at Stalingrad, there was no chance of another push into the Caucasus in 1943 and even Hitler came to realize this after he committed 17.Armee to holding the Kuban bridgehead. Instead, Hitler's attention shifted to looking for opportunities to destroy parts of the Red Army, which von Manstein claimed was possible if Heeresgruppe Süd was given priority for reinforcements. This shift of operational focus from the Caucasus to the Kursk sector left 17.Armee without a real purpose. Stripped of some of its best divisions and last on the list for replacements, it is amazing that 17.Armee was able to fight the North Caucasus Front to a standstill until the bridgehead was finally evacuated. It is also important to note that 17.Armee's defensive achievement was done without benefit of prepared defensive positions, but rather relied upon improvised field works. The Gotenkopf Stellung or Blue Line was never more than a thin grey line of Landsers holding trenches and wooden bunkers, behind some barbed wire and mines. Yet due to the narrowness of the sector and the waterlogged nature of much of the terrain, the Kuban was peculiarly well suited for the defence.

For their part, the Soviets conducted the Kuban campaign with a stubborn tunnel vision that was reminiscent of the Western Front in 1915–16. Although repeated attempts were made to outflank 17.Armee's defences on both the Black Sea and Sea of Azov coasts, these were decidedly secondary efforts and hindered by poor inter-service coordination. Instead, the North Caucasus Front unimaginatively kept trying to bash its way through the centre of the Blue Line, relying upon mass and firepower. Lacking surprise or a decisive edge in material, Soviet offensive tactics were inadequate to overcome the German defence, although they did stress it on many occasions. By May 1943, the Soviets were playing the German game, bleeding themselves for no gain and tying down 400,000 troops in a backwater theatre. In tactical terms, the Axis achieved a defensive victory by preventing an enemy breakthrough and inflicting seven casualties upon the enemy for every one of theirs; this is the reason that Hitler authorized a Kuban shield. Yet attrition-based victories tend to leave a sour taste even in the victor's mouths, particularly when followed by a withdrawal. From the Soviet perspective, the Kuban was a painful and frustrating experience with few moments to rejoice.

It is noteworthy that the campaign in the Kuban was heavily shaped by air and naval capabilities, which was unusual for the Eastern Front.

If nothing else, the Kuban campaign is memorable as one of only six campaigns during World War II for which the Wehrmacht issued a campaign shield. Hitler did not authorize the shield until 20 September 1943, when the Kuban was already being evacuated. Only about one in five of the men who served in the Kuban ever received this shield and it was more of a propaganda ploy than to honour the men of 17.Armee. Hitler wanted to make the Kuban campaign appear to have been worthwhile with this kind of heroic symbology, rather than as a serious mistake on his part. (Author's collection)

Unlike other sectors of the front where air activity was spread over a very wide area, in the Kuban air operations were concentrated in a 40 x 20km rectangular box over Krymskaya and Myskhako, which resulted in an unusually high number of dogfights and interceptions. In the Kuban, airpower proved as decisive as it did in Normandy in 1944, because it was massed over small corps-size battlefields. At times during the April and May 1943 fighting, the three divisions in Gruppe Angelis were receiving nearly as much Luftwaffe support as all of Heeresgruppe Süd would receive during Operation *Zitadelle* in July. Likewise, the VVS committed enormous resources to the Kuban, although it proved far less beneficial. Naval capability also shaped the campaign. The Germans were never able to prevent the Soviets from gradually pushing troops and equipment into the Malaya Zemlya beachhead or to sever the 18th Army's maritime supply. However, the Kriegsmarine's ability to keep 17.Armee supplied across the Kerch Strait in the face of persistent air attacks, mines and naval raids was phenomenal. In the end, the Kriegsmarine succeeded in evacuating 17.Armee intact from the Kuban – an achievement that ranks alongside the Dunkirk evacuation in both scale and impact. Had the Kriegsmarine failed, the loss of 200,000 German troops in the Kuban would have been another catastrophe like Stalingrad. Of course, the Wehrmacht was already on the path to defeat and the belated evacuation of 17.Armee from the Kuban came too late to alter that trajectory, but the troops saved did help von Manstein make a temporary stand along the Dnepr in the winter of 1943/44.

In the long run, the enduring lesson that the Kuban campaign teaches is that in war, lives and resources should not be wasted on efforts that do not contribute to victory. The Red Army suffered 471,932 casualties in the Kuban including over 119,000 dead or missing but achieved very little; the resources invested here – particularly the airpower – could have been better utilized elsewhere. While the Axis losses were much less – the Germans suffered a total of 57,499 casualties (including 15,499 dead or missing) plus 9,668 Romanian casualties (including 2,404 dead or missing) – 17.Armee was wasted in the Kuban. Hitler learned nothing from the Kuban experience and repeated this mistake again by leaving 200,000 German troops from 16.Armee and 18.Armee in the isolated Courland Peninsula in 1944–45, with the Kriegsmarine again tasked with supplying a complete army by sea. Rather than simply sealing off the Courland Pocket, the Soviets launched six offensives in six months in order to destroy the trapped German armies, but repeatedly failed and suffered over 200,000 casualties in the process.

THE BATTLEFIELD TODAY

Anyone interested in seeing the battlefields of the Kuban first-hand will find the experience challenging, but not impossible. While there are battlefield tour organizations for foreign tourists in Russia, none visit the Kuban region, so it might prove to be something of an expedition. The Kuban is still a remote area, mostly dominated by Russian oil companies and the fishing industry. In many towns, freshly polished statues of Lenin still stand, as if nothing has changed in decades. A working knowledge of Russian and finding a local guide are essential prerequisites. Flights to Krasnodar International Airport (KRR) are primarily limited to Aeroflot and other Russian-flagged carriers through Moscow, but Austrian Airlines offers a direct flight from Vienna to Krasnodar. Further potential difficulties for tourism arise from the tense security situation in the region, in part caused by the internal security threat from local factions such as Chechen and pro-ISIL terrorists and in part due to the recent Russian–Ukrainian border conflict and the seizure of the Crimea in 2014. The Caucasus is still a heavily militarized area and a Russian fighter-bomber regiment, equipped with Flankers, is stationed at the airbase north of Krymskaya.

Coastal Battery No. 394 at the port of Gelendzhik is open to tourists today. During the Kuban campaign, most of the Soviet reinforcements to the Malaya Zemlya embarked at this port and there were frequent clashes at night offshore between German S-boats and Soviet torpedo cutters. (Author's collection)

The 1950s-vintage light cruiser *Mikhail Kutuzov* is a museum ship in Novorossiysk today. This image further shows the dominant high ground around the port, which frustrated the Soviet 18th Army for so long. (Author's collection)

Tourists would be well advised to make their base of operations in Krasnodar for sight-seeing in the Kuban, with day trips to Novorossiysk, the Krymskaya area and Anapa. Krasnodar offers major hotels and car rental from Western vendors at the airport. In Krasnodar, the Museum of Military Technologies has a large amount of World War II hardware on display, including tanks and self-propelled guns (T-34s, IS-2, Su-100), artillery (76.2mm up to 203mm), infantry weapons and the rusting hulk of the *M-261*, a 1955-vintage Quebec-class diesel submarine. Like most Russian military museums, much of the equipment is anachronistic and only limited, sanitized information is presented about military campaigns.

Novorossiysk offers far fewer (and worse) hotels but is much closer to the actual battlefields of the Kuban, particularly the Malaya Zemlya. The Memorial Park Malaya Zemlya, which is located at the site of Major Kunikov's landing in February 1943, is the locus in Novorossiysk for commemorating the Kuban campaign, although mostly focused on just this aspect. In the post-war era, the Soviet State created a whole mythology about the heroism and sacrifices in the Malaya Zemlya and the ethos and artefacts of this backwater of the war are still being employed to energize Russian patriotism. Novorossiysk has plenty of other military-related sites, including the 1954-vintage light cruiser *Mikhail Kutuzov*, which is a museum ship in the harbour and open to tourists. There is also a state-run historical museum, which has displays related to World War II, plus the ruins of the Palace of Culture and a nearby monument to where the German advance was halted in September 1942. Other monuments scattered about the city include a torpedo boat, an Il-2 Sturmovik, sailor memorials and, of course, Leonid Brezhnev. Visitors should note that few, if any foreign-language guides are available in any of these sites. One new monument in the city commemorates 'the Fallen in the Undeclared War' which lists the names – but no dates – of local soldiers killed during the recent conflict with Ukraine.

On Hill 121.4 near the village of Novyy, where so much of the fighting occurred between May and August 1943, there is a memorial complex known as the 'Hill of Heroes', done in typical Soviet style, with a T-34/85 and a pair of ZIS-3 anti-tank guns mounted on plinths and adorned with red stars. A large statue of a Red Army soldier dominates the memorial. Yet aside from a few plaques with names of heroes, there is little effort to depict what actually happened here in 1943. Instead, the emphasis is on winning the war, not liberating the Kuban. As usual in Russia, there is a great deal of both authorized and unauthorized digging to unearth World War II remains and artefacts. In June 2012, the remains of 282 Soviet soldiers discovered by local Kuban clubs were re-interned at the Hill of Heroes.

There are still a few World War II bunkers in the Kuban, mostly hidden by tangled overgrowth, but Hitler's vaunted 'Blue Line' has disappeared. In Krasnyy Oktyabr, there is a simple monument to the soldiers, sailors and airmen who broke through the Blue Line in September 1943. Some coastal defences in the Taman Peninsula are still extant, but quite out of the way. Likewise, the Lagoon area remains a remote wilderness area of reed-filled marshes, with only the occasional fishing village. The continuous combat in this area has left few visible marks, although doubtless a considerable amount of the war's detritus lies just out of sight in the marshes. Near Temryuk, the hulks of sunken landing craft are still visible at low tide. Temryuk has some military displays, including a Soviet motor torpedo boat. Further south, the port of Gelendzhik was the departure point for many of the troops heading to the Malaya Zemlya and was also the scene of naval combat between light forces from both sides. Coastal Battery No. 394 is still extant and open to tourists, with both army and naval ordnance on display. Despite the lack of battlefield remains, World War II is evident everywhere in the Kuban, particularly in the small towns. In Anastasiyevskaya, there is a memorial complex for the fallen, including one to an aircrew that rammed and destroyed a German He-111 bomber. In Krymskaya, there is a poignant monument with the figure of a grief-stricken mother, listing names of local casualties.

Major Kunikov's grave in Novorossiysk. (Author's collection)

FURTHER READING

Primary sources

Captured German reports held by the National Archives and Records Administration (NARA) in College Park, MD:

17.Armee (Ia, Ic, O. Qu.) from January to June 1943: T312, Rolls 716, 717, 720, 722, 724

V Armeekorps (Ia, Ic) from January to June 1943: T314, Rolls 261, 263

XXXXIV Armeekorps (Ia) from January to June 1943: T314, Roll 1048

XXXXIX Gebirgskorps (Ia, KTB) from January to June 1943: T314, Roll 1218

13.Panzer-Division (Ia, KTB): T315, Roll 644

50.Infanterie-Division (Ia, Ic): T315, Roll 950

73.Infanterie-Division (Ia, Kriegstagebuch Nr. 10, January to June 1943): T-315, Roll 1067

97.Jäger-Division (Ia reports), March to May 1943: T315, Roll 1194

Secondary sources

Achkasov, V. I and N. B. Pavlovich, *Soviet Naval Operations in the Great Patriotic War 1941–45* (Annapolis, MD: Naval Institute Press, 1981)

Glantz, David M., *Forgotten Battles of the German-Soviet War 1941–1945*, Volume V (Self-published, 2000)

Goncharov, Vladislav et al, *Desanty Velikoy Otechestvennoy voyny (sbornik)* [*Landings of World War II*] (Moscow: Eksmo, 2015)

Gorshkov, Sergey G., *Na yuzhnom primorskom flange* [*On the Southern Flank of the Seaside, Fall 1941–Spring 1944*] (Moscow: Military Publishing, 1989)

Grechko, Andrei A., *Bitva za Kavkaz* [*Battle for the Caucasus*] (Moscow: Military Publishing, 1967)

Hake, Friedrich von, *Der Schicksalsweg der 13. Panzer-Division 1939–1945* [*The Destiny of the 13. Panzer-Division*] (Eggolsheim, Germany: Dorfler im Nebel Verlag, 2006)

Kolomiets, Maksim I., *Tanki Lend-Liza* [*Lend-Lease Tanks*] (Moscow: Eksprint, 2000)

Laskin, Ivan A., *U Volgi i na Kubani* [*In the Volga and the Kuban*] (Moscow: Military Publishing, 1986)

Mezhiritsky, Petr Y., *Tovarishch mayor* [*Comrade Major: The Life of Hero of the Soviet Union T. L. Kunikova*] (Moscow: Politizdat, 1975)

Morzik, Fritz, *German Air Force Airlift Operations* (Honolulu: University Press of the Pacific, 2002)

Moshchanskiy, Ivan and V. Stoyanov, 'Breakthrough of the "Blue Line": The Novorossiysk–Taman Strategic Offensive Operation (10 September–9 October 1943)', *Voyennaya letopis* [*The Military Annals*], 3 (2004)

Pickert, Wolfgang, *Vom Kuban-Brückenkopf bis Sewastopol: Flakartillerie im Verband der 17.Armee* (Vowinckel, 1955)

Shiian, I. S., *Ratnyi podvig Novorossiiska* [*Feat of Arms at Novorossiysk*] (Moscow: Voenizdat, 1977)

Shtemenko, Sergei M., *The Soviet General Staff at War 1941–1945* (Honolulu, Hawaii: University Press of the Pacific, 2001)

Tieke, Wilhelm, *The Caucasus and the Oil: The German-Soviet War in the Caucasus 1942/43* (Winnipeg, Canada: J. J. Fedorowicz Publishing Inc., 1995)

Tyulenev, Ivan V., *Cherez Tri Voyny* [*Through Three Wars*] (Moscow: Military Publishing, 1960)

Zhabkin, Ivan, 'Forgotten Campaign: The Caucasus', in *History of the Second World War* (Marshall Cavendish, 1973), pp. 1,457–61

Zhiltsova, Elena and Vasily Stoyanov, *Na Kubanskom platsdarme: tankovyye boi na Kubani, 5 fevralya–9 sentyabrya 1943 goda* [*On the Kuban Bridgehead: Tank Battles in the Kuban, 5 February–9 September 1943*] (BTV-MN, 2002)